"Christian family devotions—regular, simple, shared Bible times around the table—are a precious challenge throughout the seasons of family life. The what and how of starting (or re-starting!) can be the first hurdle. Ed Drew to the rescue! *The Wonder of Easter* makes it so easy for families to plunge together into the Bible, with a series of family devotions that are accessible (10 minutes, 5 per week), realistic (key studies highlighted for when you miss some), flexible (pre-school to teen options) and biblical (built around Luke's Gospel.) Open this book after dinner tonight and head off with your family on a day-by-day shared Bible adventure of your own that will, by God's grace, shape the hearts and lives of a generation."

COLIN BUCHANAN, Singer/songwriter; Presenter; Author

"Without fuss or labor, *The Wonder of Easter* deftly guides families through Jesus' last days, with both Old Testament and New Testament references. I'm grateful to Ed Drew for creating such a rich resource to help families like mine prepare our hearts for Easter and stay centered on the passion and resurrection of Jesus!"

RANDALL GOODGAME, Slugs & Bugs Family Music

"Ed Drew's awe of King Jesus fuels *The Wonder of Easter* with transformational truth. Age-specific questions and engaging activities promise to captivate the minds and hearts of every generation in your home and church. It's not just for Easter!"

BARBARA REAOCH, Director, Children's Division, Bible Study Fellowship; Author, *A Jesus Christmas; Why Christmas?* and *Why Easter?*

"The death and resurrection of Jesus are the very heart of the Christian faith. This engaging new resource will help families hear the Easter story together from Luke's Gospel. It is biblically faithful, easy for parents to use, and will enable the whole family to delight in the wonder of what God has done for us through Jesus. An ideal way to start, restart or refresh daily family devotions."

JOHN STEVENS, National Director, Fellowship of Independent Evangelical Churches in the UK

"Ed Drew has written a highly readable, brilliantly accessible resource for families. The questions are on point; and the activities are fun and engaging, and illuminate the meaning of the text. If you are looking for a Bible study to help you do devotions with your family, look no further."

JOSH MOODY, Senior Pastor, College Church, Wheaton, Illinois

"Wow! What a fantastic resource for any family who want to spend time together looking at the Easter narrative, and to help one another grow in understanding and love of their Saviour. Each session helpfully digs into Scripture and is interactive, creative and fun. The variety of questions and flexibility of the devotions mean that even the busiest family with the widest age-range of children will be able to get lots out of them. I'm totally going to be recommending this to families I know!"

TAMAR POLLARD, Author, *Epic Explorers* and *One Day Wonders Books 1 and 2*

"Christian families of all stages and sizes (including Christian adults living together) will benefit from Ed's help in re-living the Easter story together. I'll be buying copies for my godchildren and strongly recommending this fantastic resource to our church family."

ED SHAW, Pastor, Emmanuel City Centre, Bristol

"Clear, simple and full of top tips to make your family's experience of Easter all about Jesus!" Not only will this book help you unpack Luke's account of Jesus' death and resurrection; it will also equip you in knowing how to pray and read the Bible with your children for future family devotion times. Buy one for your family and another one for a friend!"

JO-ANNE TAYLOR, Children's Worker, St. Stephen's, Cape Town

"Family devotions are not easy, but Ed Drew has made them easier. This book is biblically faithful, creative, extendable for a wide age-range and time-saving! Buy it, use it and see your family transformed though God's word this Easter."

GARETH CRISPIN, Co-author, *Together With God*

"Biblical, practical, easy to use and fun. This will really help you and your kids to understand and apply the message of Easter."

MURRAY ANDERSON, Senior Pastor, St Peters Fish Hoek, Cape Town

"What an excellent resource. I will not only be buying this for family and friends and my godchildren but also encouraging Christ Church Kensington's families to buy it and use it. Although the studies are short, don't be fooled; each one gets to the main point of the passage in a way that will engage children and excite them about God's word. A great resource for families from 'Faith in Kids' to enable young and old alike to rejoice in Christ's death and resurrection. It deserves to be widely used."

MARK O'DONOGHUE, Vicar, Christ Church, Kensington

Ed Drew

An Easter journey
for the whole family

The Wonder of Easter
© Faith in Kids 2019. Reprinted 2019, 2020, 2021.
www.faithinkids.org

faith in kids

Published by:
The Good Book Company

thegoodbook
COMPANY

thegoodbook.com | thegoodbook.co.uk
thegoodbook.com.au | thegoodbook.co.nz | thegoodbook.co.in

ISBN: 9781784983352 | Printed in India

Design by André Parker

Contents

Before you begin

Easter can be the highlight of the year.

Better than Christmas.

Bigger than a birthday.

And about so much more than just chocolate.

We are going to walk through Luke's Gospel and parts of the Old Testament to discover why the story of Jesus' death and resurrection is the most amazing story ever told.

Discover a new story every day as you follow in Jesus' footsteps:

- *Shout* as Jesus rides on a donkey into Jerusalem as the returning King.

- *Listen* as an innocent man is sentenced to the ultimate punishment.

- *Mourn* as the King of the universe dies.

- *Share* the relief of knowing that Christ's pain brings us into his kingdom.

- *Watch* as the King rises again.

- *Imagine* the hill outside Jerusalem as the disciples watch their best friend rise to rule in heaven.

- *Discover* the greatest story of human history.

This is the wonder of Easter.

WHAT YOU CAN EXPECT

Take ten minutes with your family each day to prepare for Easter.

Whether your youngest is three years old or your oldest is eighteen, this flexible, easy-to-use resource will allow the whole family to celebrate the limitless wonder of Easter.

The devotions we've created are an achievable joy, not an unrealistic burden. No more than ten minutes are needed to complete a daily section. If you want to take longer, that's great!

There are five for each week. If you can't get to do this every day, that's alright. Stuff happens. We hope that if you miss one, you can pick it up again easily. You might discover that five a week is an unrealistic target. So to help you, some have been marked with "Key Story" to help you choose which ones to pick. You can also see the key stories on the chart opposite.

If you'd like a bit more help...

- there are some top tips on page 119 at the back of the book.
- there's also a Bible timeline on page 117 to help your family see how each Bible story fits into the big picture of Bible history.
- and if you would find it helpful, you can download an answer sheet to all of the questions from **www.thegoodbook.com/wonder-answers.pdf**

	MON	TUE	WED	THU	FRI	SAT	SUN
WK 1		**Shrove Tuesday** Get started early over a pancake!	**Day 1** Lk 19 v 30, 35-40	**Day 2** Zech 9 v 9-10	**Day 3** Lk 19 v 45-48		
WK 2	**Day 4** Lk 22 v 1-6	**Day 5** Lk 22 v 7-16	**Day 6** Lk 22 v 19-20	**Day 7** Ex 12 v 21-28	**Day 8** Lk 22 v 31-34		
WK 3	**Day 9** Lk 22 v 39-42	**Day 10** Lk 22 v 47-54	**Day 11** Lk 22 v 54-62	**Day 12** Lk 22 v 63-65	**Day 13** Lk 22 v 66 – 23 v 1		
WK 4	**Day 14** Lk 23 v 1-4	**Day 15** Lk 23 v 13-14, 20-25	**Day 16** Lk 23 v 32-34	**Day 17** Is 53 v 5-7	**Day 18** Lk 23 v 35-39		
WK 5	**Day 19** Lk 23 v 39-43	**Day 20** Lk 23 v 44-45	**Day 21** Ps 22 v 6-8, 16-18, 27	**Day 22** Lk 23 v 46-49	**Day 23** Lk 23 v 50-56		
WK 6	**Day 24** Ps 31 v 5, 11-16	**Day 25** Lk 24 v 1-8	**Day 26** Lk 24 v 9-12	**Day 27** Lk 24 v 13-24	**Day 28** Lk 24 v 25-35		
WK 7	**Day 29** Dan 7 v 13-14	**Day 30** Lk 24 v 36-43	**Day 31** Lk 24 v 44-49	**Day 32** Lk 24 v 50-53	**Day 33** *Good Friday* Lk 23 v 36-38		**Day 34** *Easter Sunday* Lk 24 v 1-8

Note: The **key stories** are the ones with a grey background.

Key Story

DAY 1

The return of the King

Where are we going today?

Jesus arrived in Jerusalem as God's King coming home, but some people were angry because they thought Jesus was just an ordinary man.

READY?

- **Optional.** If you are going to act out today's story, grab a bunch of coats.

- Open your Bible to **Luke 19 v 30 and 35-40** (or read the passage from page 12).

LET'S GO!

Pray: Dear Father, please help us to understand better who Jesus is so that we are most excited about him. Amen.

Passage

- *Where are we in the Bible?* Jesus is arriving in Jerusalem as the King. Since he was last here, things have changed: everyone now knows about him. It's as if Jesus has returned to Jerusalem, the capital city, to be crowned as King.

- *Look out* for how people are feeling in this true story. Watch out—there's more than one answer!

- *Read* the passage.

11

Luke 19 v 30 and 35-40

³⁰ He said, "Go into the town you can see there. When you enter it, you will find a colt tied there. No one has ever ridden this colt. Untie it, and bring it here to me.

³⁵ So they brought it to Jesus. They threw their coats on the colt's back and put Jesus on it. ³⁶ As Jesus rode toward Jerusalem, the followers spread their coats on the road before him.

³⁷ Jesus was coming close to Jerusalem. He was already near the bottom of the Mount of Olives. The whole crowd of followers was very happy. They began shouting praise to God for all the powerful works they had seen. They said,

> ³⁸ "God bless the king who comes in the name of the Lord!
> There is peace in heaven and glory to God!"

³⁹ Some of the Pharisees said to Jesus, "Teacher, tell your followers not to say these things!"

⁴⁰ But Jesus answered, "I tell you, if my followers don't say these things, then the stones will cry out."

Perhaps try...

- Act out the scene. (For under-5s, open up a pre-school Bible such as *The Beginner's Bible* for this story instead.)

- Can one of you be Jesus? Throw a coat over a chair, a buggy, a scooter or anything that can be sat on. One of you can be Jesus, sitting, as he arrives in Jerusalem—or just leave the chair empty, imagining that Jesus is there.

  The rest of you can throw your coats on the floor in front of Jesus. Praise God with the words from verse 38. Can you put these shouts into your own words? There is real joy here. God's King has finally arrived—home with his people! What would *you* have shouted if you were this excited?

Questions for us all

1. How did the crowd feel as Jesus arrived? Why did they feel like that? (See verses 37-38.)

2. How did the Pharisees feel? (See verse 39.) Why was that, do you think?

> **Know the word?**
>
> A **Pharisee** was a religious leader. They were very well-known, and respected for their knowledge and love of God. But perhaps they didn't love God as much as they thought...

Question for 3s and 4s

Did you spot what Jesus was riding on?

Question for 5-7s

Imagine being so excited about a man that you shout, sing and dance in the street as he rides past! Is there anything you know about Jesus that would make you shout and sing and dance?

Question for over-7s

In verse 40, Jesus says that if the Pharisees silence the crowds, "then the stones will cry out". Was he serious? Could anything make stones cry out?

Question for teens

What were the Pharisees feeling? (It's quite complex.) Can you suggest two or three different things that are going on in their heads? Why might people today want to shut down those who are talking about how great Jesus is?

Prayer suggestion

If you were in the crowd shouting praises to God with total joy for Jesus, what would you love to shout? If shouting out a prayer is too strange, then just say it as a quiet prayer.

Got time to chat?

Do you ever see others wanting to silence talk of Jesus—refusing to let him be mentioned in a conversation? Talking as if he's really awkward or different? Even if no one in the world was talking about Jesus, the stones could cry out in praise! Knowing this, when people don't want you to talk about Jesus, how does that change how you feel about him?

Something more for the adults?

Read Luke 19 v 41-44. How was Jesus feeling? What caused that? But the crowd had just been praising God for his arrival... so what did Jesus want for Jerusalem? And us?

DAY 2

Promised: the donkey-riding King

Where are we going today?

500 years earlier, God had promised Zechariah that he was going to send a King. Jesus is that promised King, who rode on a donkey.

READY?

- *Before you start,* turn to the timeline on page 117 to see where Zechariah fits in. We're jumping into the Old Testament to understand why Jesus rode into Jerusalem on a donkey.

- Open up your Bible to **Zechariah 9 v 9-10** (or read the passage from page 15).

- **Optional!** Write these two verses on a piece of paper to scribble notes on with a felt-tip pen. For under-7s, just stick to verse 9. Or you can write on the passage in this book opposite.

LET'S GO!

Pray: Dear Father, please help us to understand how the Bible fits together and shows us Jesus. Amen.

Passage

- *Where are we in the Bible?* This is the prophet Zechariah—we can call him Zek. Prophets were like God's postmen. When God had a message for his people, he gave it to his prophet to deliver to his people. Zek was God's postman 500 years before Jesus was born. He lived at a time when God's people had been allowed back to Jerusalem, after 70 years of being kept away. When Zek and God's people came back, Jerusalem was in ruins. There was no wall to protect them, no roofs on their houses and no temple to worship God. How do you think they felt? What do you think they would have said to God in prayer, through their tears?

We're now going to read part of God's message to his people that Zek delivered. It's a promise from God—about a time when they wouldn't feel so alone and hopeless.

- *Look out* for what this message from God reminds you of.

- *Read* the passage. For under-7s, just read verse 9.

Zechariah 9 v 9-10

⁹ Rejoice, people of Jerusalem.
    Shout for joy, people of Jerusalem.
Your king is coming to you.
    He does what is right, and he saves.
    He is gentle and riding on a donkey.
    He is on the colt of a donkey.
¹⁰ I will take away the chariots from Ephraim
    and the horses from Jerusalem.
    The bows used in war will be broken.
The king will talk to the nations about peace.
    His kingdom will go from sea to sea,
    and from the Euphrates River to the ends of the earth.

Perhaps try...

- You can circle the words as you talk about them, or write brief notes next to key phrases.

Questions for us all

1. This promise is about a King. What do we learn about this King? For each answer, can you explain what it means or put it into your own words?

2. What does this promise remind you of? Do you remember what we saw on Day 1?

Question for 3s and 4s

Imagine if you came home after a holiday and your house had no roof, and everything in your house was broken or missing. How would you feel?

Question for 5-7s

Jesus is this King in Zek's message. What do you think is the best thing about this promised King from Zek's message: that he does what is right, that he saves, or that he is gentle? Do you think Jesus is like that?

Question for over-7s

So the crowd in Jerusalem have waited 500 years for this promise to happen. As Jesus arrives on a colt, he is showing that he is the King from Zek's promise. What was there in this promise that you think they would have most looked forward to?

Question for teens

If an ordinary guy arrived in your local town riding on a donkey and saying he's the King, people in the streets would laugh him out of town. We don't expect people with real power to ride on a donkey! But the people who saw Jesus arrive that way knew Zek's prophecy. How do you think that impacted how the crowd felt about Jesus?

Prayer suggestion

What is the best news in Zek's prophecy? Thank God that *Jesus* is that best news.

Got time to chat?

When Zek looked at Jerusalem, God seemed to be a million miles away because he didn't appear to be looking after his people. Isn't God in charge of every moment of every day of every year? But he didn't appear to have been busy looking after their capital city. Does Zek's prophecy (and Jesus arriving to fulfil it) help us when we can't see God at work? How?

Something more for the adults?

There's a lot to celebrate in these two verses! Go through them one sentence at a time, and turn them into prayers of praise for Jesus Christ, who fulfils each and every one of these attributes. Pick one attribute or verse and meditate on it. When in Christ's life did he fulfil it? How does he fulfil it today? Celebrate him.

DAY 3
Clearing out the temple

Where are we going today?

Jesus did a good thing by clearing the temple of traders—but the religious leaders hated him for it.

READY?

- **Optional!** You could collect some unbreakable objects that can be swept off a table. Have you got a children's table or a chair that can be thrown over? Or could you get hold of a parent's small change?

- Open your Bible to **Luke 19 v 45-48** (or read the passage from page 18).

LET'S GO!

Pray: *The prayer is deliberately further down today.*

Passage

- *Where are we in the Bible?* In Luke's Gospel, this comes right after Jesus arrived in Jerusalem on a donkey as King. It's as if he got off his donkey and walked straight into the temple...

- *Look out* for what Jesus did, for what the religious leaders thought, and for how the people felt.

- *Read* the passage.

Luke 19 v 45-48

⁴⁵ *Jesus went into the Temple. He began to throw out the people who were selling things there.* ⁴⁶ *He said, "It is written in the Scriptures, 'My Temple will be a house where people will pray.' But you have changed it into a 'hideout for robbers'!"*

⁴⁷ *Jesus taught in the Temple every day. The leading priests, the teachers of the law, and some of the leaders of the people wanted to kill Jesus.* ⁴⁸ *But all the people were listening closely to him and were interested in all the things he said. So the leading priests, the teachers of the law, and the leaders did not know how they could kill him.*

Perhaps try...

- To bring the event to life, a child could clear the room of everyone else.

- Say, with anger, "Get out! This should be a place where anyone can talk to God, but you're using it to take people's money!" Throw over a chair, sweep some unbreakable objects off a table and send some coins flying. Those being driven out can try to grab their money and possessions on their way, in a fluster.

> **Is it ever right to be angry?**
>
> This is a rare moment when we see Jesus angry. Sometimes it is right to be angry. Jesus wasn't losing his temper. Jesus was rightfully angry about how his Father's house was being used.

Pray: *(Praying now might help to restore calm!)* Dear Father, please help us to understand why Jesus was so angry. Amen.

Questions for us all

1. Why was Jesus so angry? (See verse 46.)

2. What did the religious leaders think? When they saw Jesus clearing the temple, what did they want to do to him? (Look for the answer in verses 47-48.)

Question for 3s and 4s

Did you hear what Jesus did? What happened?

Question for 5-7s

If you had been standing there, seeing Jesus throw tables around, driving animals out, and shouting at people, what do you think you would have said about Jesus?

Question for over-7s

Why do you think the religious leaders hated Jesus so much for clearing the temple? (That's a hard question!)

Question for teens

Jesus only did good things. So clearing the temple must have been a good thing to do because he was always perfect, like his Father God. How could doing a good thing cause the leaders to want to kill Jesus?

Prayer suggestion

Pray that we would be people who love everything that Jesus says and does, just as the crowd did.

Got time to chat?

This passage reminds us that Jesus Christ makes some people absolutely furious. They want to stop anyone from hearing his words. Have you ever seen anyone behave like that? Can you imagine what it would look like if they did? What would they say? Why would they feel like that?

Something more for the adults?

Jesus is prompting the crowd to answer the question: what is real worship? The crowd thought that buying and selling animals in the temple for sacrifice was real worship. Jesus passionately disagrees with that answer! What does real worship of Jesus Christ look like for us? Does this passage help you to answer the question?

DAY 4

All against Jesus

Where are we going today?

Jesus knew that he was in the middle of a fight between good and evil, but he carried on.

READY?

- **Do it if you can!** Grab a packet of pasta. It would be great to have a couple of dozen objects that could be used to represent people. Pasta works well for this, or you can use Lego people or anything else you can find!

- Open your Bible to **Luke 22 v 1-6** (or read the passage from page 21).

LET'S GO!

Pray: Dear Father, please help us to listen carefully to what you are saying to us in the Bible. We really want to understand it, but please help us when we find that difficult. Amen.

Passage

- *Where are we in the Bible?* Jesus had been teaching at the temple every day. The crowd flocked to listen to Jesus, but the religious leaders hated him and wanted to get rid of him.

- *Look out* for who is *against* Jesus in this passage.

- *Read* the passage.

Luke 22 v 1-6

[1] *It was almost time for the Jewish Feast of Unleavened Bread, called the Passover Feast.* [2] *The leading priests and teachers of the law were trying to find a way to kill Jesus. But they were afraid of the people.*

[3] *One of Jesus' 12 apostles was named Judas Iscariot. Satan entered Judas, and he went to* [4] *the leading priests and some of the soldiers who guarded the Temple. He talked to them about a way to give Jesus to them.* [5] *They were pleased and promised to give Judas money.* [6] *Judas agreed. Then he waited for the best time to turn Jesus over to them without the crowd knowing it.*

Perhaps try...

- On your table split your pasta pieces or toy people into two groups. One group will be Jesus and those who followed him; we'll call this group "those *for* Jesus". The other group will be those who hated him and wanted him dead; we'll call this group "those *against* Jesus".

- Place "Jesus" at the head of "those for Jesus". Then there were Jesus' twelve disciples, whom Jesus had chosen, who followed him everywhere as his closest friends. Place this group just behind Jesus.

- Place "those against Jesus" separate from "those for Jesus" on the table.

Questions for us all

1. Who were the people who were against Jesus? (If you're using pasta/toy people, point to some in the group of "those against Jesus" as you answer this question.)

2. What group did Judas belong in? What did he decide to do? (If you're using pasta/toys, move one of your "people" from one group to the other.)

Question for 3s and 4s

Jesus looked after his followers. They were his friends. Do you want Jesus to look after you? (*Note: This passage calls Jesus' closest followers his apostles, but do say "disciples" if your children would find that easier.*)

Question for 5-7s

What was Judas given to make him want to change sides?

Question for over-7s

Those against Jesus were powerful and rich and there were a lot of them. But Jesus wasn't worried or scared. Why do you think that was?

Question for teens

Why is the devil getting involved? What does that tell you about Jesus, the religious leaders and these particular events?

Prayer suggestion

Thank God that Jesus wasn't surprised or worried by the enemies he had. Thank God for who Jesus is—the one with all power, all control, and all goodness, who can stand against all evil.

Got time to chat?

It helps us to understand how important the first Easter was when we see the gathering enemies against Jesus. It was a real-life cosmic war—one never to be repeated. How does that help us when we come across evil or hatred that scare us today?

Something more for the adults?

None of us enjoy having enemies or being isolated by others. Jesus knew that plans for his murder were developing and that his friend was betraying him. So why would Jesus carry on, without changing his plans, without seeking to compromise, without running away? It's because of his love for me and you.

A note about Satan

We don't usually talk to children about the devil/Satan, so it may feel strange or awkward hearing about him in this passage. Here are a few pointers that might help.

- Satan is the not the hero of this story or any other story in the Bible. So it would be a shame if he got discussed more than Jesus today.

- Jesus always beat the devil whenever he met him. So we do not need to be scared or worried about him.

- The Bible does say that Satan is real. "Satan" means "enemy"—that's all he is. When Jesus died on the cross, Satan was beaten (Colossians 2 v 15), so that anyone who puts their trust in Jesus is completely safe. So we can be certain that we are totally safe from the devil and his power.

- In this story, "Satan entered Judas", meaning that Satan was now changing Judas' choices. Judas was working for Satan.

DAY 5

Just as Jesus said

Where are we going today?

Jesus knew every detail of how Peter and John would find a room for the Last Supper, because he knew every detail of what was about to happen.

READY?

- **Optional!** Grab a piece of paper and some pens or pencils.
- Open your Bible to **Luke 22 v 7-16** (or read the passage from below).

LET'S GO!

Pray: Dear Father, please help each of us to get to know Jesus better from today's passage. Amen.

Passage

- *Where are we in the Bible?* Judas went to the religious leaders who were planning to kill Jesus. Judas said he wanted to help them.
- *Look out* for what Jesus said would happen, and then what actually happened.
- *Read* the passage.

Luke 22 v 7-16

⁷ The Day of Unleavened Bread came. This was the day the Passover lambs had to be sacrificed. ⁸ Jesus said to Peter and John, "Go and prepare the Passover meal for us to eat."

⁹ They asked, "Where do you want us to prepare it?"

*Jesus said to them, ¹⁰ "Listen! After you go into the city, you will see a man carrying a jar of water. Follow him into the house that he enters.
¹¹ Tell the person who owns that house, 'The Teacher asks that you please show us the room where he and his followers may eat the Passover meal.'
¹² Then he will show you a large room upstairs. This room is ready for you. Prepare the Passover meal there."*

¹³ So Peter and John left. Everything happened as Jesus had said. So they prepared the Passover meal.

*¹⁴ When the time came, Jesus and the apostles were sitting at the table.
¹⁵ He said to them, "I wanted very much to eat this Passover meal with you before I die. ¹⁶ I will never eat another Passover meal until it is given its true meaning in the kingdom of God."*

Perhaps try...

- Can the children sketch Jesus' words to Peter and John, as he explains what they will find as they go into Jerusalem? (See verses 10-12.)

Questions for us all

1. Jesus told Peter and John what would happen when they went looking for a place to have their Passover meal. How close was Jesus to knowing what actually happened to Peter and John?

2. How could Jesus get it exactly right?

Question for 3s and 4s

Jesus told Peter and John to find a man carrying a... what?

Question for 5-7s

Can you remember what Jesus got exactly right? Can you list the details?

Question for over-7s

We call this meal "the Last Supper". It was a very special meal. What clues are there that it was special for Jesus?

Question for teens

Jesus said that he had been really looking forward to eating this meal with his friends before he died. Why do you think that was? What was there to look forward to, when he knew that awful suffering was coming?

Prayer suggestion

What is surprising or amazing about Jesus in this story? If you know, then tell him! Let's pray.

Got time to chat?

How do you see Jesus' love for people in this story? Here we see how much Jesus delights to be with his friends. Can you imagine Jesus loving you? He knows you as an individual. He knows your name, what you hate, what you're frightened of, what makes you laugh... When would it help you to remember this?

Something more for the adults?

Imagine Jesus had sat down with *you* at that meal and said, *You've no idea how much I have looked forward to eating this Passover meal with you before I enter my time of suffering.* How would you feel? What would you want to say to him? Amazingly, you will be able to tell him yourself when you see him at the final party meal in the new creation.

DAY 6

Body and blood

Where are we going today?

Jesus changed the Passover meal so that his friends would understand why he had to die.

READY?

- **Do it if you can!** Have some bread ready and a glass of purple juice (or water with some red food colouring).
- Open your Bible to **Luke 22 v 19-20** (or read the passage from below).

LET'S GO!

Pray: Dear Father, as we read what Jesus said when he was explaining why he was about to die, help us to understand what he meant. Amen.

Passage

- *Where are we in the Bible?* Jesus was sitting down to the meal he had looked forward to for so long—the special last meal with his friends.
- *Look out* for how Jesus used the bread and wine to explain to his friends why he was choosing to die.
- *Read* the passage.

Luke 22 v 19-20

¹⁹ Then Jesus took some bread. He thanked God for it, broke it, and gave it to the apostles. Then Jesus said, "This bread is my body that I am giving for you. Do this to remember me." [20] *In the same way, after supper, Jesus took the cup and said, "This cup shows the new agreement that God makes with his people. This new agreement begins with my blood which is poured out for you."*

Perhaps try...

- Use real bread and a purple drink to experience something of what Jesus was explaining.
- Break your bread and pass it around as you say Jesus' words in verse 19.
- Pass the purple drink around, each sharing the same cup, as you say Jesus' words in verse 20.

Questions for us all

1. What did Jesus say the bread was like?
2. What did Jesus say the red wine was like?

Question for 3s and 4s

Have you noticed what colour blood is? *(Parents—help your young children see that blood is a little like the colour of red wine or purple juice. That's why Jesus said his blood is like the wine.)*

Question for 5-7s

Did you notice who Jesus said his body would be broken for and who his blood would be spilt for?

Question for over-7s

What do you want to remember about Jesus from this story? Why do you want to remember this?

Question for teens

"Agreement" or "covenant" in verse 20 means "promise". This is a binding promise that God will never break. The cup of red wine reminds us of Jesus' promise to keep us safe. It sounds so strange to us, but can you think why blood might be used as a sign of a promise to keep another person safe?

Prayer suggestion

Imagine you had been sitting at that table. Jesus was asking that his followers eat bread and drink wine to remember his life, which he was about to give for them. If you'd been there, what would you have wanted to say to him? Please say that to him, right now, because right at this moment he is closer to you than he was to his disciples at that meal.

Got time to chat?

Ever feel unloved? Alone? Jesus sat next to his friends and told those he loved that he would lay down his life for them. He says the same to us. How does that feel, to know there is someone (and not just anyone!) who has laid down his life for you? How can that help when we feel unloved?

Something more for the adults?

Read Luke 22 v 21. It's amazing that we read in verses next to each other that Jesus is about to give himself (verses 19-20) and that someone is about to betray him (verse 21). Giving himself, while being handed over—at the same time. His life freely given—yet taken from him. The perfect gift—yet the worst betrayal. Grace offered—yet sinfully demanded.

DAY 7
Like the lamb

Where are we going today?

Jesus died at Passover time to show us that he is our Passover Lamb, who died to keep us safe.

READY?

- We are jumping back into the Old Testament to understand how Jews in Jesus' day (and still in our day) remembered the meaning of the Passover. Then we will understand how Jesus changed its meaning so that we would remember the meaning of his death.

- **Do it if you can!** Find some brown card— the inside of a cereal box will work. Cut out three rough rectangles. Two will be the same size—longer to be the uprights of a doorframe. The third will be shorter to be the cross piece of the doorframe.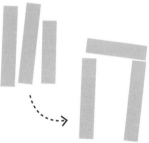

- On the next page, we show how they can become a cross instead.

- Find some red paint or tomato ketchup. Put a little of either in a pot so that the imagination can allow it to represent blood.

- Find a small object that can be used to represent a person. Use a toy figure, a cork with a face drawn on it or any photo cut out of a magazine.

- Have the timeline ready (page 117) to show when in history this story happened.

- Open your Bible to **Exodus 12 v 21-28** (or read the passage from below).

LET'S GO!

Pray: Dear Father, we really want to understand how the whole Bible fits together and shows us Jesus. Please help us to do that today. Amen.

Passage

- *Where are we in the Bible?* We read in Luke 22 v 15, "I wanted very much to eat this Passover meal with you before I die". We are going to understand what the Passover meal was, so that we can understand why Jesus chose to die.

- *Explain* (using the Bible timeline, page 117). We are going back more than a thousand years before Jesus was born, to a time when God's chosen people were slaves in Egypt, under a cruel Pharaoh (or king). God told Pharaoh to let his people go free. Pharaoh refused. God sent ten plagues to punish Pharaoh and to show who the real boss was. After nine plagues, Pharaoh still would not obey God and let his people go. So it was time for the terrible tenth plague…

- *Look out* for the job of the Passover lamb.

- *Read* the passage.

Exodus 12 v 21-28 (Good News Translation)

21 Moses called for all the leaders of Israel and said to them, "Each of you is to choose a lamb or a young goat and kill it, so that your families can celebrate Passover. 22 Take a sprig of hyssop, dip it in the bowl containing the animal's blood, and wipe the blood on the doorposts and the beam above the door of your house. Not one of you is to leave the house until morning. 23 When the LORD goes through Egypt to kill the Egyptians, he will see the blood on the beams and the doorposts and will not let the Angel of Death enter your houses and kill you. 24 You and your children must obey these rules for ever. 25 When you enter the land that the LORD has promised to give you, you must perform this ritual. 26 When your children ask you, 'What does this ritual mean?' 27 you will answer, 'It is the sacrifice of Passover to honour the LORD, because he passed over the houses of the Israelites in Egypt. He killed the Egyptians, but spared us.'"

The Israelites knelt down and worshipped. 28 Then they went and did what the LORD had commanded Moses and Aaron.

Perhaps try...

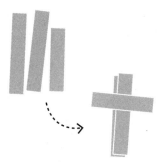

- Lay the three pieces of card on a table top, to form a rough doorframe. As you talk about the lamb dying and its blood being spread on the doorframe, you can smear some paint or ketchup on the doorframe. Place the toy person inside the door frame. Show how the destroyer *passed over* each door marked with a lamb's blood.

- When you come to talk about Jesus' death as our Passover lamb, place the two uprights one on top of the other, and move the cross-piece down over the uprights, so that you now have a cross shape. Place the toy person under one arm of the cross. Show how God's punishment on us *passed over* those trusting in Jesus' blood, shed at the cross.

Questions for us all

1. What happened to the Passover lamb? (See verses 21-22.)

2. Why did the people have to do this? (See verse 23.)

Question for 3s and 4s

God looked after his people in this story. Did you hear what animal he used to look after them?

Question for 5-7s

God had made a promise that his people would be safe because a lamb had died instead of them. How would the Angel of Death (also called the destroyer) know which houses to keep safe?

Question for over-7s

How is Jesus *our* Passover lamb? What happened to him that is like the first Passover lambs?

Question for teens

In verses 24-27, we discover that God told his people to keep celebrating this event with an annual ceremony. When Jewish children asked why they were still doing it, did you hear what the parents should say? (See verse 27.) "Sacrifice" means "one dies in the place of another". Imagine that you are explaining this to a friend who finds all this bloodthirsty and weird. What would you say?

Prayer suggestion

Jesus sat down to celebrate the Passover, knowing he was going to be the new Passover lamb. You could either say sorry for your sin, which meant that he needed to die for you, or you could thank him for being your Passover lamb.

Got time to chat?

Sometimes we all wonder if God really will keep us safe; if we really are trusting; if our faith is real. From today's story, what made God's people certain they were safe? What makes *us* certain we are safe?

Something more for the adults?

Read on through verses 29-30. There is a stark difference between those houses marked with the blood and those without: total safety and total despair.

DAY 8

Peter's big claim

Where are we going today?

Jesus knew that Peter was about to say, three times, that he never knew him. Jesus still made sure that Peter was safe in his family for ever.

READY?

- **Optional!** Did you do Day 4's devotion (page 20)? It was the one where Judas agreed to betray Jesus—with the two sets of people: those *for* Jesus and those *against* Jesus? Whether you did or not, bring out a couple of dozen objects that can be used to represent people. Grab some pasta shells, or use Lego people.

- Open your Bible to **Luke 22 v 31-34** (or read the passage from page 34).

LET'S GO!

Pray: Dear Father, thank you that we can read your Bible, understand what it means and be changed by your Spirit to be more like Jesus. Amen.

Passage

- *Where are we in the Bible?* Jesus is sitting with his closest friends, enjoying the special Passover meal. It's the night before his death.

- *Look out* for which side you think Peter is on. Confusingly in this story, he is called both Simon *and* Peter. It's the same man!

- *Read* the passage.

Luke 22 v 31-34

[31] *"Satan has asked to test all of you as a farmer tests his wheat. Simon, Simon,* [32] *I have prayed that you will not lose your faith! Help your brothers be stronger when you come back to me."*

[33] *But Peter said to Jesus, "Lord, I am ready to go to prison with you. I will even die with you!"*

[34] *But Jesus said, "Peter, before the cock crows tonight, you will say you don't know me. You will say this three times!"*

Perhaps try...

- On a table top, split your toy people or pasta shapes into two groups. One group will be led by Jesus with those who followed him. We'll call this group "those *for* Jesus". The other group will be those who hated him and wanted him dead. We'll call this group "those *against* Jesus".

- In "those for Jesus", there is Jesus and his twelve disciples, whom Jesus had chosen, who followed him everywhere as his closest friends. Place this group just behind Jesus.

- Leave "those against Jesus" a little separate from "those for Jesus".

Questions for us all

1. What did *Peter* say he was ready to do? Why do you think he said that? (Look in verse 33.)

2. What did *Jesus* say Peter would do that day? (Look in verse 34.)

A note about Jesus keeping people safe

Today's devotion may lead to a question about why Judas wasn't kept safe from Satan but Peter was. There is no need to raise this unless a child does. There are some answers we can give but it is a hard question:

- Let's not think that *we* are brave enough or good enough. Only *Jesus* is strong enough to keep us safe.

- Jesus is always stronger than Satan. Jesus let Satan take Judas, but Jesus chose to keep Peter safe.

- Judas decided to hate Jesus and plan to kill him. Let's be careful not to be like Judas. Instead, let's trust Jesus to hold us.

- We don't need to be afraid of making mistakes, like Peter's. Jesus will always keep us safe.

Question for 3s and 4s

Did Peter know Jesus?

Question for 5-7s

Peter said that he would do *anything* for Jesus. But Jesus said that Peter would lie and say that he didn't know Jesus at all. Who do you think was right?

Question for over-7s

Jesus said that he had prayed for Peter so that Peter would keep trusting Jesus (in verse 32). *(If you're using toys/pasta, point to the Peter character in the "those for Jesus" group.)* Jesus had prayed that Peter would always stay in this group. Who kept Peter in this group? Was it Peter or Jesus?

Question for teens

Jesus tells Peter that Satan wants to test Peter. Do you think Jesus wants to frighten Peter, reassure him, make him feel guilty, or just tell him what's happening?

Prayer suggestion

When would it help you to know that Jesus is in charge of everything that will happen? Thank Jesus that we can trust him to be in charge. Thank him that he can keep us safe.

Got time to chat?

Children can have their mistakes pointed out to them daily. Sometimes they feel crushed, maybe as Peter did. In those moments, what could they remember from this story to encourage them to keep going, with hope?

Something more for the adults?

We know the disappointment and regret we feel when we see our mistakes. Read Romans 8 v 31-35. What is true for Peter is also true for us. Jesus is praying for you. You're safe!

Advance warning!

The next family Bible time features an activity with a mug full of burning paper. Your children might enjoy the thrill of fire in their kitchen and they might understand more of the Bible story as a result. If this is an activity that you want to attempt, you may want to take a look at the activity before you sit down with your children for that Bible time.

DAY 9

Drinking from the worst cup

Where are we going today?

Jesus prayed that he would not be punished on the cross for all of our sins—but he also said that he would do what his Father in heaven wanted him to.

READY?

- **Do it if you can!** Get a cup or mug, some pens, several small pieces of paper and some matches. Loosely scrunch up some newspaper in the bottom of the cup, so that it is about half full. You might be having a small fire in the cup, so pick an old one that is fireproof!

- Instead of fire, you could use a paper shredder.

- Open your Bible to **Luke 22 v 39-42** (or read the passage from page 37).

LET'S GO!

Pray: Dear Father, please help us to think about the things we have done wrong. We often don't like admitting wrong things, so please help us. Amen.

Passage

- *Where are we in the Bible?* Jesus has just finished his special Passover meal. He gets up, leaves the room and goes, with his disciples, to a quiet place on the Mount of Olives.

- *Explain that...*

  - Jesus talks about a "cup" in this story. It's not a real cup. It's picture language for the right anger that we deserve for all our sin.

  - Instead of just holding a few of our sins, imagine this cup had *all* of the sins we've ever done and God's anger. Now imagine it had in it *all* the anger at *everyone's* sins! Now imagine that drinking this cup meant taking all of God's anger, all of the fair punishment for sin. It's a terrible thought.

- *Look out* for what Jesus prayed would happen to this cup.

- *Read* the passage.

Luke 22 v 39-42

39-40 Jesus left the city and went to the Mount of Olives. His followers went with him. (Jesus went there often.) He said to his followers, "Pray for strength against temptation."

41 Then Jesus went about a stone's throw away from them. He kneeled down and prayed, 42 "Father, if it is what you want, then let me not have this cup of suffering. But do what you want, not what I want."

Perhaps try...

- Using small pieces of paper, each person in the family (including adults) can write or draw one thing they have done wrong. No one will to have to show anyone else these pieces of paper (though to keep things concrete for the youngest children, any 3- or 4-year-olds will be asked later what theirs was).

- Then turn the pieces of paper over and write "God's anger" or draw something to show "anger". Each thing we do wrong is one more way of saying to God, "**S**hove off God. **I** want to be in charge. **N**o to living your way." These choices cause our loving Father in heaven to feel angry at how we are treating him and others, and even ourselves.

- Fold up the pieces of paper and put them all into the one cup. Make sure that some of the pieces are not folded flat. There needs to be some air between the pieces of paper.

Questions for us all

1. What did Jesus ask his Father in heaven for?

2. Do you know what happened to all of God's anger when Jesus died on the cross? So think about the sins we've written down and put in the cup—if we're trusting Christ, what's happened to them?

   - *Jesus was punished for all these sins. All the anger was placed on Jesus. So there's no sin left; no anger left; no punishment left.*

   - *With due precaution, **set fire to the paper in the cup OR shred it!** (If burning, tilt the cup sideways so that you can light the newspaper at the bottom; then all the slips of paper should burn as well.)*

Question for 3s and 4s

Did you think of something that you had done wrong? Can you tell us what it was?

Question for 5-7s

What's left of the mistakes and wrong things you drew on your piece of paper? *(This is true of our sins even if the bits of paper aren't burnt or shredded.)*

Question for over-7s

Jesus asked God not to punish him for all of our sins, but also said he would do what God wanted. How did God answer that prayer? Why do you think that was?

Question for teens

Why did Jesus ask God to take away the cup? Surely Jesus was perfect, so why was it an issue for him?

Prayer suggestion

Say sorry to Jesus for the wrong things you've done or thank Jesus that he took them away.

Got time to chat?

Some children seem crushed by the wrong things they do. If so, here is an opportunity to talk about the relief Jesus offers. Other children seem to barely notice the wrong things they do. If so, here is an opportunity to talk about how we know that those things matter.

Something more for the adults?

Read Luke 22 v 43-46. These verses give a rare insight: where we see a little of the courage it took to take the cup. Jesus took it out of love. *For you.*

> **Note for parents: What is "the cup"?**
>
> Isaiah 51 v 17 shows that "the cup" is an illustration to help us understand what it means to be punished for our sin. God is rightly angry when we treat him and others badly. His anger can be pictured as a cup full of punishment that deserves to be drunk by the one who has sinned. It is a really unpleasant and painful image to think about—and that's why Jesus was in anguish when he thought about "drinking" it for us. It's also another way of helping us to understand and appreciate Jesus' incredible act of love by dying on the cross.

Key Story

DAY 10
Taken away by guards

Where are we going today?

Judas, who had pretended to be Jesus' friend, came with soldiers to arrest him. Jesus was still kind and gentle, and in control.

READY?

- **Optional!** Can you find an object to use as a sword that wouldn't hurt if someone got hit with it, such as a drinking straw or a card sword.
- Open your Bible to **Luke 22 v 47-54** (or read the passage from page 40).

LET'S GO!

Pray: Dear Father, hearing you talk to us in the Bible is more exciting than a king or queen chatting to us in person. Thank you! Amen.

Perhaps try...

- This is a very physical passage. One of you can read the passage and give instructions to anyone else available, so that they can act it out.
- Make sure you have the following in the drama: a kiss, a sword swipe, a cut-off ear, a healed ear and an arrest.

Passage

- *Where are we in the Bible?* Judas has already told the religious leaders that he will hand Jesus over to them, to have him killed. Jesus is on the Mount of Olives with his friends, where he's gone to pray.

- *Look out* for the fight. What does Jesus do?

- *Read* the passage.

Luke 22 v 47-54

[47] *While Jesus was speaking, a crowd came up. One of the 12 apostles was leading them. He was Judas. He came close to Jesus so that he could kiss him.*

[48] *But Jesus said to him, "Judas, are you using the kiss to give the Son of Man to his enemies?"*

[49] *The followers of Jesus were standing there too. They saw what was happening. They said to Jesus, "Lord, should we use our swords?"* [50] *And one of them did use his sword. He cut off the right ear of the servant of the high priest.*

[51] *Jesus said, "Stop!" Then he touched the servant's ear and healed him.*

[52] *Those who came to arrest Jesus were the leading priests, the soldiers who guarded the Temple, and the Jewish elders. Jesus said to them, "Why did you come out here with swords and sticks? Do you think I am a criminal?* [53] *I was with you every day in the Temple. Why didn't you try to arrest me there? But this is your time—the time when darkness rules."*

[54] *They arrested Jesus and took him away. They brought him into the house of the high priest. Peter followed them, but he did not go near Jesus.*

Questions for us all

1. What happened during the fight?

2. Jesus told them that they could have arrested him on any day. Why do you think they came with soldiers and swords at night time?

Question for 3s and 4s

Did you hear who the soldiers came to get?

Question for 5-7s

Jesus is so powerful that he could have flicked the soldiers down the hill with just his little finger. He could have uprooted a tree, swung it like a club and whacked the whole crowd who came to get him. Why didn't he?

Question for over-7s

Judas chose to hand Jesus over to the soldiers with a kiss. Why do you think Jesus was sad about that?

Question for teens

Jesus knew exactly why his enemies hadn't arrested him during the day, while he taught in the temple. He told them, "But this is your time—the time when darkness rules." What do you think Jesus meant by that?

Prayer suggestion

What surprises you about Jesus in this story? How does that make you think about him? Thank Jesus that this is what he is like.

Got time to chat?

On the news, in our country and even in the place where we live, we see evil. Just like in this story, Jesus is allowing evil to rule in some places for some time. Can you see that Jesus is still in charge even though the soldiers arrest him and take him away? When we see evil ruling, what should we remember? What can we pray?

Something more for the adults?

When we see evil, when we see intimidating strength, but when we struggle to see it clearly because it's hidden in the shadows of the darkness—how do we respond? How do we feel? We are not Jesus. We do not have his courage, his strength or his control. So what is the right response for someone who is trusting in Christ, in those moments.

DAY 11
All alone

Where are we going today?

Jesus knew that he would be left alone by his friends. He was so brave.

READY?

- **Optional!** Grab a bin (to use as a pretend fire) and three different hats.

- Open your Bible to **Luke 22 v 54-62** (or read the passage from page 43).

LET'S GO!

Pray: Dear Father, please can your Holy Spirit help us to understand what you want to teach us from this part of the Bible. Amen.

Perhaps try...

- Place the bin in the middle of the room. You're going to pretend it's a fire to warm your hands during a cold evening outdoors. You could go outside with the bin to help you to feel what it might have been like.

- Place some chairs around the "fire".

- In this story, it is a different person each time who asks Peter if he knows Jesus, so put a different hat on each time a new person speaks.

- One or more of you could practise saying, "I don't know Jesus". Say this every time Peter replies to a question.

Passage

- *Where are we in the Bible?* During dinner Peter had said he was ready to follow Jesus to prison and death (verse 33). Jesus replied that before the cock crowed, Peter would say three times that he didn't even know Jesus.

- *Look out* for what Peter said when he was asked about Jesus.

- *Read* the passage. Allow the children to say Peter's lines or "I don't know Jesus" each time.

Luke 22 v 54-62

⁵⁴ *They arrested Jesus and took him away. They brought him into the house of the high priest. Peter followed them, but he did not go near Jesus.*

⁵⁵ *The soldiers started a fire in the middle of the courtyard and sat together. Peter sat with them.* ⁵⁶ *A servant girl saw Peter sitting there near the light. She looked closely at Peter's face and said, "This man was also with him!"*

⁵⁷ *But Peter said this was not true. He said, "Girl, I don't know him."*

⁵⁸ *A short time later, another person saw Peter and said, "You are also one of them."*

But Peter said, "Man, I am not!"

⁵⁹ *About an hour later, another man insisted, "It is true! This man was with him. He is from Galilee!"*

⁶⁰ *But Peter said, "Man, I don't know what you are talking about!"*

Immediately, while Peter was still speaking, a cock crowed. ⁶¹ *Then the Lord turned and looked straight at Peter. And Peter remembered what the Lord had said: "Before the cock crows tonight, you will say three times that you don't know me."* ⁶² *Then Peter went outside and cried with much pain in his heart.*

Questions for us all

1. Each person told Peter something different: *This man was with Jesus, You are one of Jesus' group* and *This man was with Jesus; he's from Galilee.* What did Peter say each time?

2. Afterwards, there was a moment when Jesus looked at Peter, just after the cock crowed. Maybe it was through a window or as they took Jesus from one part of the house to another. How did Peter feel?

Question for 3s and 4s

What was Peter doing while these people spoke to him?

Question for 5-7s

Earlier that day *Peter* had said he would follow Jesus to prison. *Jesus* told Peter that he would say he didn't even know Jesus—three times, before the cock crowed. Who got it right? And did either of them get it *exactly* right?

Question for over-7s

Why do you think Peter said three times that he didn't know Jesus? Are you ever tempted to pretend you don't know Jesus?

Question for teens

Jesus knew that Peter was going to say three times that he didn't know Jesus. Since Jesus knew what was going to happen, do you think that means he didn't mind when it did happen?

Prayer suggestion

Jesus knew and understood exactly how Peter would behave—better than Peter did. Give thanks that Jesus was taken by soldiers and left alone by his friends *for us*.

Got time to chat?

We don't need to be as brave, as wise, or as powerful as Jesus. He has that covered. When you next feel that you've let Jesus down, what would you love to remember or say to yourself or to Jesus?

Something more for the adults?

As we read verse 62, "Then Peter went outside and cried with much pain in his heart," we can feel the brokenness, the regret and the shame. He remembered Jesus' words predicting that he would fail in exactly this way. Somehow, the prediction of failure makes it all the worse.

Would Peter also remember Jesus' words in verse 32: "But I have prayed that you will not lose your faith"? Jesus knew failure would come, but he would also be there for Peter, to strengthen him afterwards. Thank Jesus that his grace will always be sufficient for you in your failure and brokenness. He is not surprised. He will not deny you. He will strengthen you.

DAY 12

Bullied, beaten and laughed at

Where are we going today?

The soldiers who hurt Jesus and laughed at his weakness were actually part of King Jesus' plan.

READY?

- **Optional!** Find a blindfold—perhaps a kitchen towel or a scarf.
- Open your Bible to **Luke 22 v 63-65** (or read the passage from below).

LET'S GO!

Pray: Dear Father, please help us to understand why people wanted to hurt and laugh at Jesus. Amen.

Passage

- *Where are we in the Bible?* Jesus has been arrested by soldiers. He is at the house of the religious leaders. His friends have left him. Peter even said he didn't know Jesus.
- *Look out* for what the soldiers did to Jesus.
- *Read* the passage.

Luke 22 v 63-65

63-64 Some men were guarding Jesus. They made fun of him like this: They covered his eyes so that he could not see them. Then they hit him and said, "Prove that you are a prophet, and tell us who hit you!" [65] *The men said many cruel things to Jesus.*

Perhaps try...

- Play a game to find out a little of how it felt for Jesus:
- One member of the family can be blindfolded and stood in the middle of the room.
- Others can move around and gently poke the blindfolded person. Each time, the blindfolded person has to guess who poked them or where that person is in the room.
- How does it feel to be blindfolded? It's fun when you feel safe and know that those around you will look after you.
- Jesus wasn't allowed to take off the blindfold. His hands were tied. He didn't feel safe. It wasn't a game. No one was looking after him. The soldiers didn't poke him—they hit him. Over and over again. Laughing. Shouting. Hurting. Beating. It was horrible.

Questions for us all

1. What did the soldiers do to Jesus? There are about four or five different things if you look carefully. Do you know what each one means?
2. Why do you think they were making fun of Jesus? What was it about him that they wanted to make fun of?

Question for 3s and 4s

No one should make fun of someone else or hit them. How do you think that made Jesus feel?

Question for 5-7s

If Jesus had wanted to, could he have escaped? What could he have done to the soldiers? Was a blindfold any use with Jesus?

Question for over-7s

Why do you think Jesus chose to let the soldiers hurt him? Why didn't he tell them who was hitting him?

Question for teens

Look back at Luke 18 v 31-32. What did Jesus say would happen? The soldiers wanted Jesus to prophesy. But by hitting Jesus and shouting, "Prove that you are a prophet" at him, what did the soldiers actually prove about Jesus? Wrap your head around that!

Prayer suggestion

Is there something that you would like to say to Jesus right now? You can say that to him.

Got time to chat?

We sometimes look at what is happening to us and say, "God couldn't bring anything good out of this". Perhaps there is hurt and loneliness, or sadness, or confusion, or evil. It is such a mess that we want to shout at God, "You don't know what you are doing. Things are out of control. You're not in charge." That's really what the soldiers were shouting at Jesus. We sometimes need to understand the same thing that the soldiers needed to understand. What is that?

Something more for the adults?

Read Isaiah 50 v 6-7. These are subtitles to this event. This is the mind of Christ. Praise him for his infinite wisdom, patience and power.

Key Story

DAY 13
I Am

Where are we going today?

Jesus said that he was the Son of God, the promised King who will rule from God's throne. The religious leaders hated him for saying that.

READY?

- **Optional!** Get a sheet of paper or card and draw a table like this:

- For younger ones who can't read, just have the first column with one big red cross.

- Open your Bible to **Luke 22 v 66 – 23 v 1** (or read the passage from page 49).

Jesus on trial—the judge's verdict

Things Jesus did wrong:	Punishment Jesus deserves:
v 69:	
v 70:	

LET'S GO!

Pray: Dear Father, help us today to see clearly that Jesus really is the Son of God. Amen.

Passage

- *Where are we in the Bible?* The day before had been a busy day for Jesus. He'd eaten his last meal with his friends, followed by prayer on the Mount of Olives. He was arrested there by soldiers and dragged off to the religious leaders for a night of beatings and questioning. This story is early the next morning.

- *Look out* for whether you think the trial is fair.
- *Read* the passage. If you have more than one reader, two different people could read for Jesus and "the judges" (which is all the other spoken words).

Luke 22 v 66 – 23 v 1

22 v 66 When day came, the elders of the people, the leading priests, and the teachers of the law came together. They led Jesus away to their highest court. *67* They said, "If you are the Christ, then tell us that you are!"

Jesus said to them, "If I tell you I am the Christ, you will not believe me. *68* And if I ask you, you will not answer. *69* But beginning now, the Son of Man will sit at the right hand of the powerful God."

70 They all said, "Then are you the Son of God?"

Jesus said to them, "Yes, you are right when you say that I am."

71 They said, "Why do we need witnesses now? We ourselves heard him say this!"

23 v 1 Then the whole group stood up and led Jesus to Pilate.

Perhaps try...

- It is hard to understand what happens in a law court or a trial.
- This table (see opposite) might help us to understand what is happening in this story.

Questions for us all

1. What did Jesus say about himself?

2. Why did the religious leaders think Jesus should be punished? If you're using the chart, can you put down what the judge would have written on his table? *(Note: This is what Jesus' enemies thought about Jesus. They thought he was wrong when he said the things he did. But Jesus never did anything wrong—not one thing!)*

Question for 3s and 4s

The men in the story were shouting at Jesus. Were they happy or angry?

Question for 5-7s

What did Jesus say about himself that made the religious leaders so angry?

Question for over-7s

What was wrong with the way Jesus was treated?

Question for teens

What is it about saying, "I'm the Son of God" that would make so many people so angry?

Prayer suggestion

Jesus is the Son of God, seated at the right hand of God the Father in heaven. He is the King and boss of the world, and he has God's power. He is pretty awesome! Take it in turns to pray, each beginning your prayer with "Lord, you are awesome because…"

Got time to chat?

Next time there is wilful disobedience or deliberate wrong behaviour, take the opportunity to remember the one we serve who is seated on his throne in glory, exactly as he predicted. He is the one we serve. He is the one we trust. He is the one we obey. It's still hard work to live for him rather than for ourselves. Pray about it.

Something more for the adults?

The religious leaders were so angry because they thought Jesus was dragging the Lord God down to the level of a bruised, chained, arrogant rebel. Read Colossians 1 v 15-23. Jesus was telling the truth all along. He is the powerful Son of God, elevated to the right hand of God. What reasons can you find to praise the Son of God today?

DAY 14

He has done nothing wrong

Where are we going today?

Jesus stood quietly as the King, while the religious leaders treated him unfairly. Pilate, the Roman Governor, knew the truth.

READY?

- **Optional!** You're going to play a gentle game of catch so find a ball or a soft object to throw.
- Open your Bible to **Luke 23 v 1-4** (or read the passage from page 52).

LET'S GO!

Pray: Dear Father, it is sad when people are treated unfairly or left out. It is surprising to see a King treated that way. Please teach us why Jesus let that happen to him. Amen.

Perhaps try...

- Have a game of piggy-in-the-middle. To play this, one person, the piggy, sits in the middle while a ball is thrown around them. If you're playing inside, the piggy just watches the ball. If it's safe, the piggy can try to get the ball while the other players try to keep it from the piggy. If there are just two of you, one person can throw the ball to themselves, while the piggy watches: it's a lonely experience!
- In today's story, Jesus was treated like the piggy in a game of piggy-in-the-middle. Everyone else was allowed to do what they wanted, while he was left to watch. It was unfair and unkind.

Passage

- *Where are we in the Bible?* The religious leaders have decided that Jesus must be punished with death for saying that he is the Son of God. But they're not allowed to punish him, so they send him to the Roman Governor (like the Prime Minister or President), hoping that he will punish Jesus with death. The Governor's name is Pilate. Don't get confused—he's not the pilot of a plane!

- *Look out* for the one question Jesus was asked.

- *Read* the passage.

Luke 23 v 1-4

¹ *Then the whole group stood up and led Jesus to Pilate.* ² *They began to accuse Jesus. They told Pilate, "We caught this man telling things that were confusing our people. He says that we should not pay taxes to Caesar. He calls himself the Christ, a king."*

³ *Pilate asked Jesus, "Are you the king of the Jews?"*

Jesus answered, "Yes, that is right."

⁴ *Pilate said to the leading priests and the people, "I find nothing wrong with this man."*

Questions for us all

1. What did the religious leaders say about Jesus?

2. What was the one question Jesus was asked?

Question for 3s and 4s

Jesus didn't say very much. Pilate asked him, "Are you the king?" Listen to whether he says yes or no. (Read verse 3.)

Question for 5-7s

These people told Pilate lies about Jesus. He hadn't said not to pay taxes. In fact he had said the opposite. They twisted what Jesus said. He wasn't confusing the people—he was trying to teach them the truth. And Jesus said he was the King, because he was! If you had been in the room, what would you have wanted to say to Pilate?

Question for over-7s

The Roman Governor, Pilate, said this about Jesus: "I find nothing wrong with this man". If Pilate was taking a test on Jesus and he gave that answer, what mark out of 10 would you give him? Why?

Question for teens

Jesus stayed silent. When he was asked a question, he gave a short answer. He didn't argue. He didn't fight. Do you think he was weak? How would you describe him?

Prayer suggestion

Thank God for what you have learned about Jesus from this story. Pray for yourself to learn something from how Jesus behaves.

Got time to chat?

Jesus shows us how to behave when we are treated unfairly or teased, or people tell lies about us. He kept quiet. He was never unkind. He told the truth. He remembered who he was. He could do all of this because he trusted his Father in heaven to be in charge for his good, always. If we tried to be like that, what part would we find hardest?

Something more for the adults?

Let's take two of the accusations made against Jesus by the religious leaders:

1. "We caught this man telling things that were confusing our people."

2. "He calls himself the Christ, a king."

What is the truth in each of these accusations? If Jesus had been asked to reply to these accusations, what do you think he might have said? What will you say to him now in prayer? Can you find one reason to thank him and one point of prayer for yourself?

DAY 15

Kill him!
Kill him!

Where are we going today?

Jesus had broken no laws, but the crowd shouted for Jesus' death until Pilate gave in.

READY?

- **Optional!** Draw the outline of a man onto a large sheet of paper. Mark a "J" on the face. This is Jesus.

- Find two felt-tip-pens or crayons in different colours.

- Open your Bible to **Luke 23 v 13-14 and 20-25** (or read the passage from page 55).

LET'S GO!

Pray: Dear Father, as we read about people who hated Jesus, please help us to know what to think when we meet people who hate your Son. Amen.

Passage

- *Where are we in the Bible?* The religious leaders decided that Jesus deserved death for saying that he was the Son of God. Governor Pilate could find nothing wrong with him.

- *Look out* for how the crowd and Pilate think so differently about Jesus.

- *Read* the passage.

Luke 23 v 13-14 and 20-25

[13] *Pilate called all the people together with the leading priests and the Jewish leaders.* [14] *He said to them, "You brought this man to me. You said that he was making trouble among the people. But I have questioned him before you all, and I have not found him guilty of the things you say.*

[20] *Pilate wanted to let Jesus go free. So he told this to the crowd.* [21] *But they shouted again, "Kill him! Kill him on a cross!"*

[22] *A third time Pilate said to them, "Why? What wrong has he done? I can find no reason to kill him. So I will have him punished and set him free."*

[23] *But they continued to shout. They demanded that Jesus be killed on the cross. Their yelling became so loud that* [24] *Pilate decided to give them what they wanted.* [25] *They wanted Barabbas to go free, the man who was in jail for starting a riot and for murder. Pilate let Barabbas go free and gave Jesus to them to be killed.*

Perhaps try...

- *Do this activity during the questions for all.* Two of the family take a felt-tip or crayon each.
- With one colour, one person will write or draw, inside or around the outline of Jesus, what *Pilate* thought and said about Jesus.
- With the other colour, the other person will write or draw what the *crowd* and the *religious leaders* thought and said (and shouted) about Jesus.
- If there are more than two of you, then have two groups. All those in each group need similar colours.

Questions for us all

1. What did Pilate think and say about Jesus?

2. What did the crowd think of Jesus?

Question for 3s and 4s

Did you hear that the crowd were shouting? Were they shouting kind things or mean things about Jesus?

Question for 5-7s

What did the crowd want to happen to Jesus? What did they want to happen to the criminal, Barabbas?

Question for over-7s

If Pilate was so sure that Jesus had done nothing wrong, why did he send Jesus to be killed?

Question for teens

Pilate treated Jesus terribly, because the crowd were so loudly against Jesus. Sometimes we see people treat Jesus terribly in what they say about him or his followers. How does this passage help us in those moments?

Prayer suggestion

Jesus had done nothing wrong. But the crowd and Pilate stood together for evil. Thank Jesus that he stayed silent, because he had a plan to beat all evil. He was going to die for our wrong attitudes and actions.

Got time to chat?

The crowd was Jewish—God's special chosen people. They were standing looking at their forever King, and yet they screamed for his death. We join the crowd whenever we wish that Jesus wasn't ruling over us—when we wish we didn't have to live for him, serve him, or grow to be like him. In those moments, we can feel sad as we realise that we are letting Jesus down again. But we can also remember that it was for us in moments like those that Christ stayed silent.

Something more for the adults?

The thousands and thousands of voices were united as one in their desire to see Christ murdered. The crowd were made *by* Jesus, *for* Jesus. So here was creation screaming for the blood of the Creator. It is helpful to remember the tragedy of that situation, as a motivation to tell a screaming world that their Creator rose from the dead and still stands before them.

Key Story

DAY 16
Nailed to a cross

Where are we going today?

Jesus wanted his Father to forgive those who were nailing him to a cross.

READY?

- **Optional!** Get a piece of paper and some felt-tip pens. Draw the three crosses, ready for adding Jesus and the two criminals. Or create the scene using some play dough, some Lego people and ice-lolly sticks.

- Open your Bible to **Luke 23 v 32-34** (or read the passage from page 58).

LET'S GO!

Pray: Dear Father, help us to see how surprising Jesus' actions and words were, as he was nailed to a cross. Amen.

Perhaps try...

- Go through the steps of this story with drawings or toy people, as you read it.

  1. Jesus and two criminals were taken outside of Jerusalem, outside the city walls.

  2. At the place of execution, all three men were fixed to the crosses, and left to die.

3. Jesus prayed for those who were doing this to him, asking that God would forgive them. They didn't understand that they were killing the Son of God.

4. The soldiers rolled dice to see who would keep Jesus' clothes. He was so unimportant to them.

Passage

- *Where are we in the Bible?* The religious leaders had decided that Jesus should be punished with death for saying he was the Son of God. Pilate knew Jesus had done nothing to deserve death, but he gave in to the crowds and sent Jesus to his death.

- *Look out* for what happened to Jesus and what he did.

- *Read* the passage.

Luke 23 v 32-34

32 There were also two criminals led out with Jesus to be killed. 33 Jesus and the two criminals were taken to a place called the Skull. There the soldiers nailed Jesus to his cross. They also nailed the criminals to their crosses, one beside Jesus on the right and the other beside Jesus on the left. 34 Jesus said, "Father, forgive them. They don't know what they are doing." The soldiers threw lots to decide who would get his clothes.

Questions for us all

1. What are the different things that happened to Jesus in this passage?

2. How did Jesus behave during these terrible moments?

Question for 3s and 4s

The soldiers really hurt Jesus. Did you hear where they put him to die?

Question for 5-7s

The soldiers thought Jesus was just another bad man who was being punished. What did they do with his clothes?

Question for over-7s

Do you remember what Jesus prayed as he was being put on the cross? Why is this prayer surprising?

Question for teens

If you stop for a moment and consider who Jesus is, what is the most surprising part of this passage?

Prayer suggestion

Jesus never stopped being loving and kind to those he met, even those who were in charge of his death. Thank God for that incredible love and care that Jesus still shows.

Got time to chat?

Jesus prays for people who hate him. What an amazing thought! He longed for those who killed him to be forgiven and to become his brothers and sisters. Wow! Imagine how much more Jesus prays for you, who are holding tight to him. When you make a huge mistake, and you feel as if you've let down Jesus (and others), what do you want to say to yourself and to Jesus? What do you thinking Jesus is praying to his Father for you?

Something more for the adults?

Jesus' prayer for those who were crucifying him is breathtaking. How could anyone do that? How can anyone long for people such as these to join him in heaven, as his brothers and sisters? It is a mind-and-heart-expanding moment. What love! What compassion and mercy! But the moment and the prayers continue—even today. Read Romans 8 v 31-35. Don't ever doubt that you are in Christ's thoughts. He is praying for you. Don't be downcast by your sin. Don't think you should throw yourself out of the kingdom—because Christ will do everything needed to hold you tight in his kingdom. The Lord himself is praying for you. Nothing can separate you from his eternal love.

DAY 17

We are healed by his wounds

Where are we going today?

God gave Isaiah a message explaining how Jesus would silently die for the things we have done wrong.

READY?

- Turn to the timeline on page 117 to show where Isaiah comes. Isaiah wrote his prophecy many years before Jesus. It is God explaining exactly what would happen and why.

- **Do it if you can!** Find a heavy weight or a big book, for the explanation later. Have a felt-tip pen to hand.

- Open your Bible to **Isaiah 53 v 5-7** (or read the passage from page 61).

LET'S GO!

Pray: Dear Father, help us to understand the message you gave to Isaiah hundreds of years before Jesus' death. Amen.

Perhaps try...

- You can use verse 7 (and verse 5 if you want) as a checklist. As you read through the verses slowly, say whether each thing *did* happen as Isaiah said it would. Can you remember when or how it happened?

- Verse 7 works best with this approach. Verse 5 will need more explanation.

Passage

- *Where are we in the Bible?* God's people were feeling alone and cut-off from God in Babylon, a land far from their home. So God gave them this promise to encourage them. God gave this message to his prophet Isaiah to deliver to his people; Isaiah would be like a postman.

- *Look out* for how much of Jesus' trial and death is described in this prophecy.

- *Read* the passage.

Isaiah 53 v 5-7

⁵ *But he was wounded for the wrong things we did.*
   He was crushed for the evil things we did.
The punishment, which made us well, was given to him.
   And we are healed because of his wounds.
⁶ *We all have wandered away like sheep.*
   Each of us has gone his own way.
But the Lord has put on him the punishment
   for all the evil we have done.

⁷ *He was beaten down and punished.*
   But he didn't say a word.
He was like a lamb being led to be killed.
   He was quiet, as a sheep is quiet while its wool is being cut.
   He never opened his mouth.

Questions for us all

1. What did Isaiah get exactly right? How did he know what would happen hundreds of years before?

2. Read the second half of verse 6. What did God ask Jesus to do for us?

   Note: A visual aid will help with this. Write "me" on the palm of one hand and "Jesus" with a crown on the other palm. Place your heavy weight, or big book, on "me" on your open hand. This is the "punishment for all the evil we have done" (verse 6). Explain that this is what God laid on Jesus when he was on the cross. Transfer the weight from one hand (me) onto the other hand (Jesus).

Question for 3s and 4s

Jesus didn't say anything when they hurt him. That was hard for him. When you are hurting, what do you normally do?

Question for 5-7s

Jesus was like a sheep. Sheep go quietly where they're told. Where was Jesus told to go? Did he go quietly?

Question for over-7s

When you read what Isaiah said about Jesus, how do you feel about Jesus? Why do you feel like that?

Question for teens

When you read this, you see so many details that happened exactly like this. Jesus was "wounded" on the cross with nails. He was "beaten down and punished" by soldiers beating him and nailing him on the cross. And he was completely "silent" when people lied about him and when the crowd shouted at him. How does it encourage or help us that we have this promise from 700 years before it actually happened?

Prayer suggestion

Thank Jesus, who was willing to let God lay on him "the punishment for all the evil we have done".

Got time to chat?

In the details, frustrations, joys and confusion of each day, it is wonderful to know that across hundreds of years God has good plans to save and love us. We don't ignore the details of each day, but sometimes it helps us keep going through those details if we are certain that God has a perfect plan. When we feel so lost in the difficulty of a day, what shall we say to ourselves?

Something more for the adults?

We will never tire of reading Isaiah 53. Jesus knew it by heart. He grew up waiting for this prophecy to be fulfilled. How much more blessed are we than Isaiah! Where Isaiah could only look forward to what God would do, we have the full, complete, beautiful picture.

DAY 18
Save yourself

Where are we going today?

Jesus chose to stay on the cross to save us. None of the different people who shouted angrily at him understood that.

READY?

- **Optional!** In this story, there are four groups of people who each treat Jesus slightly differently. Use these pictures to focus attention on each in turn. They show:

  - the *people* who wanted to watch Jesus die.

  - the *religious leaders* who told Jesus he was a liar.

  - the *soldiers* who made fun of Jesus for saying he was a King.

  - the *criminal* who just wanted Jesus to save his life.

- Open your Bible to **Luke 23 v 35-39** (or read the passage from page 64).

LET'S GO!

Pray: Dear Father, please help us to be excited to study the Bible, even in these sad stories. Help us to keep learning more about Jesus. Amen.

Perhaps try...

- Look at each different group as we read how each responded to Jesus differently.

Passage

- *Where are we in the Bible?* Jesus has been crucified. He is on the cross dying slowly.

- *Look out* for what each group thought and said as they saw Jesus dying.

- *Read* the passage.

Luke 23 v 35-39

[35] *The people stood there watching. The leaders made fun of Jesus. They said, "If he is God's Chosen One, the Christ, then let him save himself. He saved other people, didn't he?"*

[36] *Even the soldiers made fun of him. They came to Jesus and offered him some vinegar.* [37] *They said, "If you are the king of the Jews, save yourself!"* [38] *(At the top of the cross these words were written: "THIS IS THE KING OF THE JEWS.")*

[39] *One of the criminals began to shout insults at Jesus: "Aren't you the Christ? Then save yourself! And save us too!"*

Questions for us all

1. The religious leaders shouted, "If he is God's Chosen One, the Christ, then let him save himself. He saved other people, didn't he?" How did they think Jesus could prove he really was God's promised King?

2. The soldiers shouted, "If you are the king of the Jews, save yourself!" What did the soldiers expect from a man who said that he was the king?

Question for 3s and 4s

Who shouted at Jesus while he was on the cross?

Question for 5-7s

Everyone seemed confused that Jesus had said he was the Son of God, but now he was dying on a cross. What did they think he should do?

Question for over-7s

If you had the chance to talk to all these people, what would you want to explain to them? What did they need to understand?

Question for teens

Why didn't all these people just walk away and ignore Jesus? Once he was on the cross, why do you think they hung around and shouted stuff at him?

Prayer suggestion

Jesus must have been so tempted to listen to what they shouted—and jump off the cross, and walk away. But he didn't. Thank Jesus for his self-control, love and bravery.

Got time to chat?

The criminal thought he knew exactly what he needed Jesus to do for him. It's a prayer we all want to pray—we ask Jesus to do what we want him to do. Why didn't Jesus answer the criminal's prayer? Why doesn't Jesus always do what we want him to do for us?

Something more for the adults?

Can you imagine what a modern-day equivalent is for each of these four responses? Which is most common among your friends?

DAY 19

Saved! Just in time

Where are we going today?

Jesus saved a criminal who understood that only Jesus could let him into heaven for ever with him.

READY?

- **Do it if you can!** Can you find three post-it notes or some removable labels? Masking tape would do. Or failing that, just three small pieces of paper.

- Open your Bible to **Luke 23 v 39-43** (or read the passage from page 67).

LET'S GO!

Pray: Dear Father, thank you for your amazing, mind-bendingly good news! Please help us to understand the greatest news we will ever hear. Amen.

Perhaps try...

- Use two of the post-it notes to label the two criminals, on the left and right, as *sinners*. As criminals facing this punishment, they must have been two of the worst people ever.

  - On their post-it notes, scribble a mess. What do you think they had done to make such a mess of their lives?

  - Some of their sins are the same as ours— not obeying God as their wonderful Creator, and thinking of themselves first and not others.

- Use the third post-it note to label Jesus, in the centre, as *perfect*.
  - No mess here! Draw a big crown.
  - Jesus didn't deserve any punishment, at all, ever.
  - He had loved God every moment of every day. He had loved others more than himself, always taking time to serve them. His life is not like ours!
- When you arrive at the moment when Jesus promised heaven to the second criminal, you can swap his note with Jesus' note (1 Peter 3 v 18).
  - Jesus took the criminal's punishment for every one of his sins when he died. And he takes the punishment for anyone else's sins, if they trust in him and his death for them.
  - Jesus gave his perfect life to the criminal, so that the criminal could walk into glorious, perfect heaven.

Passage

- *Where are we in the Bible?* Jesus has been put on the cross. All those standing around could not understand how it was possible that Jesus was dying like this, if he really was God's promised King. But there was one man who got it...
- *Look out* for what Jesus promised one of the criminals.
- *Read* the passage.

Luke 23 v 39-43

^{39} One of the criminals began to shout insults at Jesus: "Aren't you the Christ? Then save yourself! And save us too!"

^{40} But the other criminal stopped him. He said, "You should fear God! You are getting the same punishment as he is. ^{41} We are punished justly; we should die. But this man has done nothing wrong!" ^{42} Then this criminal said to Jesus, "Jesus, remember me when you come into your kingdom!"

^{43} Then Jesus said to him, "Listen! What I say is true: Today you will be with me in paradise!"

Questions for us all

Note: If you are doing the "Perhaps try..." suggestion using post-it notes, then you can do it before asking these questions.

1. What did this criminal understand about himself?

2. What did this criminal understand about Jesus?

Question for 3s and 4s

Did you hear what Jesus promised to the other man on the cross?

Question for 5-7s

Where is this criminal now? What do you think he is enjoying most?

Question for over-7s

Why do you think this criminal didn't ask Jesus to save him from dying on the cross?

Question for teens

Do you think it's fair that a terrible, guilty criminal is allowed into heaven? That doesn't seem right after the life he has lived, does it?

Prayer suggestion

What has surprised you most today? Thank Jesus for that. (If you're stuck, the criminal's prayer in verse 42 is pretty good.)

Got time to chat?

It's hard to imagine that God sees Jesus' perfect life when he looks at us. It doesn't feel like it. When we find it hard to believe, what can we say to ourselves to be sure that we belong in heaven now?

Something more for the adults?

Even to his last breath, Jesus amazes us. What does this last conversation teach us about him?

Advance Warning!

The next family Bible time features an activity with a curtain that needs to be torn in half. Your children might enjoy the chance to rip up some fabric, and they might understand more of the Bible story as a result. If this is an activity that you want to attempt, you might want to dig out an old piece of curtain or fabric, and then take a look at the activity before you sit down with your children for that Bible time.

Key Story

DAY 20

Darkness and a torn curtain

Where are we going today?

As Jesus took his last breath, God tore the temple curtain showing that Jesus' death could let anyone be with God.

READY?

- **Do it if you can!** You will need a chair to represent God's special room. Find a curtain, table cloth, bed sheet or just a large sheet of newspaper. Do you have an old bed sheet that you're happy to tear in half? If so, using scissors, make a short cut, half way along one side, to start the tear.

- Open your Bible to **Luke 23 v 44-45** (or read the passage from page 70).

LET'S GO!

Pray: Dear Father, as we learn more about Jesus' death, please help us to learn more about how amazing he is. Amen.

Perhaps try...

- Explain visually why God tore the temple curtain:

  - Place the chair away from you, facing you. This stands for God's special room in the temple. This room was kept only for God. People couldn't just go in there, just as we can't walk into a throne room. Hold up the curtain between you and the chair as a barrier, so that you can't see or come close to God's special room.

- We can't be with God because of our sin. The curtain reminded God's people that they couldn't be with God. They couldn't be in God's family. Their sin meant that they had to stay away from God. He was being kind by not allowing anyone in—they'd be destroyed if they came in.

- At the moment that Jesus died, God tore the curtain. If you're going to tear your sheet, now is the moment! As the sheet tears, you can now see God's special place and walk to it.

- Jesus' death has taken away our sin and given us Jesus' perfect, holy life. So now, anyone trusting in Jesus' death can come close to God. The torn curtain showed that we can now be in God's family.

Passage

- *Where are we in the Bible?* Jesus has been crucified. He is on the cross dying slowly.

- *Look out* for the two things God did to show that Jesus' death was changing everything.

- *Read* the passage.

Luke 23 v 44-45

[44] *It was about noon, and the whole land became dark until three o'clock in the afternoon.* [45] *There was no sun! The curtain in the Temple was torn into two pieces.*

Questions for us all

1. What were the two things God did to show that Jesus' death was changing everything?

2. Which of these two is the most surprising or amazing, do you think?

Question for 3s and 4s

Did you hear what God tore?

Question for 5-7s

God tore the curtain in the temple that had been blocking the way to his special room. What did God want everyone to understand?

Question for over-7s

Here are 2 facts:

a) Without Jesus' death, you could not have survived being close to God.

b) Because of Jesus' death, you can be in God's family, calling him "Dad".

Which of these two facts do you find the most surprising? Why is that?

Question for teens

Sometimes we think that we can get ourselves into God's family by doing good things, or by attending church or by some other means we can control. How does today's story help you understand the truth?

Prayer suggestion:

Jesus' death completely changes us. Everything is different. Can you think of what you most want to thank God for?

Got time to chat?

All of us sometimes feel unsure about whether we're really in God's family, whether God's family is real, and whether we'll be there in heaven. In those moments of confusion and worry, what do you want to remember about today's story?

Something more for the adults?

Read Hebrews 10 v 19-23. These aren't simple verses, but they help us understand and think more clearly about the torn curtain. Find one idea that you want to think about more.

DAY 21

Treated like a worm

Where are we going today?

Jesus' suffering was so hard for him—and was also planned.

READY?

- Turn to the timeline on page 117. This song was written years *before* Jesus. It is God explaining exactly what *will* happen and how it will feel for his King.

- Open your Bible to **Psalm 22 v 6-8, 16-18 and 27** (or read it on page 73).

LET'S GO!

Pray: Dear Father, please help us to see how King David's song helps us understand more about Jesus' death. Amen.

Perhaps try...

- Start with a game to think about today's topic.
    - One of you can pick an emotion or feeling. Now make a face to show how you feel. Can the rest of your family guess what you are feeling?
    - Each of you have a go at pretending to feel a different emotion, while the rest of your family has a chance to guess from your face.
    - Emotions you could do are anger, happiness, worry, confusion, surprise, love and fear.
- It is hard to guess how someone is feeling by looking at them. We're now going to read a song written by King David to explain how he was feeling.

Passage

- *Where are we in the Bible?* We are leaving Jesus—on the cross, outside Jerusalem—and jumping back in time 1000 years. King David was on the throne in Jerusalem. He wrote this song when he was suffering.

  - God made these things happen to King David, who wrote them down.

  - God did this so that we could read these words and understand what our better King, Jesus, suffered on the cross for us.

- *Look out* for how much of this song could have been sung by Jesus.

- *Read* the passage.

Psalm 22 v 6-8, 16-18, 27

6 But I am like a worm instead of a man.
  Men make fun of me.
  They look down on me.
7 Everyone who looks at me laughs.
  They stick out their tongues.
  They shake their heads.
8 They say, "Turn to the Lord for help.
  Maybe he will save you.
  If he likes you,
    maybe he will rescue you."

16 Evil men have surrounded me.
  Like dogs they have trapped me.
  They have bitten my arms and legs.
17 I can count all my bones.
  People look and stare at me.
18 They divided my clothes among them,
  and they threw lots for my clothing.

27 People everywhere will remember
  and will turn to the Lord.
All the families of the nations
  will worship him.

Questions for us all

1. Did you spot how many of the things that David talks about happened to Jesus?

2. What clues are there in this song that help us see how Jesus was feeling when these things were happening to him?

Question for 3s and 4s

As we read verse 7, can you do what the crowd did to Jesus? Is that a good thing to do to someone who is hurting?

Question for 5-7s

They made fun of David (in verse 8), saying, *You've trusted God to look after you; well, let's see if he rescues you now!* The people making fun of Jesus shouted just the same sort of thing. What do you think they expected God to do if he was going to rescue Jesus?

Question for over-7s

David says (in verse 6), "But I am like a worm instead of a man. Men make fun of me. They look down on me." How does he feel? How have they made him feel like that?

Question for teens

Read verse 27. What do you think it is about these events which means that when people everywhere remember them, they will turn to the Lord? Why would all families in all countries worship him?

Prayer suggestion

Jesus felt alone, in pain, laughed at and misunderstood. What would you like to say to Jesus now that you've understood that?

Got time to chat?

In verse 27 we read, "People everywhere will remember and will turn to the Lord. All the families of the nations will worship him." Do we sometimes think some people or countries don't need Jesus? Do you know much about how people in every corner of the earth have turned to the Lord?

Something more for the adults?

We have seen how hard King David found suffering. Now read Psalm 22 v 3-5 and 9-11 to see how he thought of God throughout. These sections tell us how David never lost hope in his Lord. Pick one of the reasons why King David stood firm through suffering. Can you say that for yourself? Can you say that through difficulty? Will you thank God that he will hold you through suffering?

DAY 22
He died

Where are we going today?

The battle-hardened army officer was certain Jesus was God's perfect one, as he saw Jesus die.

READY?

- **Optional!** Gather together some props or basic costumes.
  - To pretend to be the army officer, find something long and thin to use as a spear (a broom or mop) or a toy sword (an umbrella, a rolling pin or a rolled-up newspaper).
  - To pretend to be one of the people gathered to watch, find any item of clothing that is "ordinary": a cap, your coat or your school bag.
  - To pretend to be one of those who knew Jesus, find a scarf for a woman or a large coat over the shoulders for a man.
- Open your Bible to **Luke 23 v 46-49** (or read the passage from page 76).

LET'S GO!

Pray: Dear Father, please calm our hearts to think about the moment that the Son of God took his last breath. Amen.

Perhaps try...

- Read the passage; then act out each person. One person could play all the parts in turn, or give them out to the willing people you have available.

- *Jesus* (without a costume) can carefully stand on a chair. Say the line, "Father, I give you my life". Then take one last breath, drop your head as though dead and stay standing.

- *The army officer* needs to look completely shocked and blurt out, *Wow! This man really had done nothing wrong. Ever!*

- *The person from those gathered to watch* acts as though they've suddenly realised that they have made a huge mistake, and shouts, *What have we done? How did we let this happen?*, then walks away.

- *Those who knew Jesus* need to drop your heads, as though you've been completely beaten.

- Once each part has been practised, the actor(s) could run through the characters (changing costumes), as if Jesus' last breath is the gun going off to start the drama.

Passage

- *Where are we in the Bible?* Jesus has been crucified. He is on the cross dying slowly. It's been dark for three hours. The curtain has been torn. God has now switched the sun back on. Jesus is taking his final breaths…

- *Look out* for what the different people did at the moment Jesus died.

- *Read* the passage.

Luke 23 v 46-49

[46] *Jesus cried out in a loud voice, "Father, I give you my life." After Jesus said this, he died.*

[47] *The army officer there saw what happened. He praised God, saying, "I know this was a good man!"*

[48] *Many people had gathered there to watch this thing. When they saw what happened, they returned home. They beat their chests because they were so sad.* [49] *Those who were close friends of Jesus were there. Some were women who had followed Jesus from Galilee. They all stood far away from the cross and watched.*

Questions for us all

1. What do you think Jesus meant by "Father, I give you my life"? It's a strange thing to say as you're about to die.

2. Which of the people there surprise you most in what they said or did: the army officer, those people who had gathered or Jesus' friends?

Question for 3s and 4s

Jesus' friends watched Jesus die. How do you think they felt?

Question for 5-7s

The army officer was a brave soldier who had seen many people die. What did he think of Jesus?

Question for over-7s

Why do you think the army officer said what he did? What do you think convinced him?

Question for teens

It's interesting that these three people or groups of people all saw the same thing but each reacted very differently. Why do you think that is? Which of the three is the most interesting to you?

Prayer suggestion

Thank God for how Jesus died, and how he kept trusting to the very end. Or tell God how you feel as you have "watched" Jesus die.

Got time to chat?

The atmosphere of this scene is terribly sad. It is how a funeral can feel. A loved one has gone. There is sadness that we can't talk to that person anymore. It all feels hopeless. But Jesus was placing his life into his Father's hands, knowing that he would rise again on the other side of death. What a trust Jesus had in his Father! When do we feel that we want to give our lives to our loving Father in heaven? Will we remember that our lives are safe with him?

Something more for the adults?

It was Passover time. Jerusalem was full to bursting with every Jew who could fit into it. Of all the people in Jerusalem, this army officer might have been the single least likely person to understand who Jesus was. He'd probably seen *more* death on more battlefields than anyone else in Jerusalem. He'd probably been into the temple *less* than anyone else in all Jerusalem. He'd probably seen *less* of Jesus' teaching and miracles than anyone else. But he is the only person who stands at the cross and praises God. Here is a man who shows the power of the Spirit to reveal who Jesus is. See the power of the Spirit at work in a very unlikely person to bring him to praise God.

Key Story

DAY 23
Put in a tomb

Where are we going today?

We are certain that Jesus really was dead because those who put his body in the tomb were careful.

READY?

- **Optional!** To act out a little of this story, you will need a bed sheet or duvet cover. (Keep it to use on Day 26 as well.)
- Open your Bible to **Luke 23 v 50-56** (or read the passage from page 79).

LET'S GO!

Pray: Dear Father, thank you that you have allowed us to see so much of Jesus' last days. Today, please help us to be sure that he was really dead so that we can feel the miracle of his resurrection. Amen.

Perhaps try...

- Wrap one of your number in the sheet and see if you can carry them across the room. Or, you can lay a child on the sheet and lift the corners to carry him or her across the room.
- As you move a child, wrapped in cloth, talk about these next three steps. We can be certain that Joseph and the women were sure that Jesus really was dead.

  1. Could you take a body off the cross, wrap it in a sheet and carry it to a tomb, and not notice if he was still alive and breathing?

2. Could you get confused about which body was Jesus' body, if his was the only body in the tomb?

3. Could you get the wrong tomb if Joseph had put the body in there and a group of women had watched him do it?

Passage

- *Where are we in the Bible?* Jesus died on the cross. The army officer saw how Jesus died and was certain that Jesus was not a criminal but was someone very special.

- *Look out* for whether we can be sure Jesus really was dead.

- *Read* the passage.

Luke 23 v 50-56

50-51 A man from the Jewish town of Arimathea was there, too. His name was Joseph. He was a good, religious man. He wanted the kingdom of God to come. Joseph was a member of the Jewish council, but he had not agreed when the other leaders decided to kill Jesus. 52 Joseph went to Pilate to ask for the body of Jesus. 53 So Joseph took the body down from the cross and wrapped it in cloth. Then he put Jesus' body in a tomb that was cut in a wall of rock. This tomb had never been used before. 54 This was late on Preparation Day. When the sun went down, the Sabbath day would begin.

55 The women who had come from Galilee with Jesus followed Joseph. They saw the tomb and saw inside where the body of Jesus was laid. 56 Then the women left to prepare perfumes and spices.

On the Sabbath day they rested, as the law of Moses commanded.

Questions for us all

1. Can you spot the different things Joseph did that day? (Look at verses 52-53.)

2. Choose one of you to be Joseph. It could be a parent or a child. Then ask "Joseph" this question: "How can you be so certain that Jesus really was dead when you put his body in the tomb?"

Question for 3s and 4s

Listen to me reading verse 53. Can you listen for where they put Jesus' body?

Question for 5-7s

The group of women were planning to come back a few days later to finish getting Jesus' body ready to be left alone in the tomb. What did they watch and check before they went home?

Question for over-7s

How can we be certain that Jesus was really dead? How can we be sure that Jesus' friends knew exactly where his body had been left?

Question for teens

Does it matter to you that Jesus did actually die, rather than that he just fainted? Why / why not?

Prayer suggestion

Thank God that because of Joseph and the women, we can be sure that Jesus really had died.

Got time to chat?

Do the people in this passage look as if they expect Jesus to rise from the dead? In fact, Jesus had told his friends many times that he would, as in Luke 18 v 31-33. If they had been convinced Jesus would rise from the dead, what would you have expected them to do differently? As it was, they were amazed and couldn't believe it. How does this help us to trust what we read in the Gospels?

Something more for the adults?

This story is all we know about Joseph of Arimathea, though we are told the same information in the other Gospels. In these verses, we do learn enough about him to be inspired. From the council that condemned Jesus, he was the only member who disagreed with their decision. By going to Pilate, he was bravely making public his support for Jesus. He had taken Jesus at his word, trusting that the kingdom of God had arrived. What faith, courage and determination! It is amazing where you find encouraging faith in others. Pray for the Lord to continue amazing you by the faith you see in others, sometimes in surprising places.

DAY 24
the promised death

Where are we going today?

Jesus' last words were from Psalm 31. He was trusting his Father through death.

READY?

- As on Day 21, we're back with David in the Psalms.

- Prepare two pieces of paper. One has a sad face on it and the other has a happy face on it.

- Open your Bible to **Psalm 31 v 5 and 11-16** (or read the passage from page 82).

LET'S GO!

Pray: Dear Father, please let us see how King David's song helps us to understand our King. Amen.

Perhaps try...

- **Optional!** This idea needs more time and energy than usual.

- Leave a note where the rest of your family will see it. The note can say, "I love you! Get the family together and head down to _____." Perhaps send them down the garden, or to meet in the car, or to come to your bedroom, or to meet in the park. Be as daring as your family and circumstances allow. Make it a treat when they arrive. Have chocolate, drive out for ice cream or make a den to sit in.

- As you enjoy being together, explain that the rest of your family trusted that you loved them, so they did what you asked.

- King David sings in this song about trusting God, knowing he was loved. David could trust God with everything, even his life, in the hardest times.

Passage

- *Where are we in the Bible?* Jesus had just died and been buried. Do you remember Jesus' last words? He said, "Father, I give you my life". Jesus was actually saying one of the lines he had learned from one of King David's songs—Psalm 31 v 5.

- We've jumped back in time 1000 years; King David is on the throne in Jerusalem. He wrote this song when he felt alone, worried and hurting, when he was nearly dead and while people were making fun of him. Sound like anyone you know?

- *Look out* for when David's mood changes. Use your happy and sad faces. Work out which one to hold up first. Then work out when to change over from one to the other.

- *Read* the passage.

Psalm 31 v 5 and 11-16

⁵ *I give you my life.*
   Save me, Lord, God of truth.

¹¹ *Because of all my troubles, my enemies hate me.*
   Even my neighbours look down on me.
When my friends see me,
   they are afraid and run.
¹² *I am like a piece of a broken pot.*
   I am forgotten as if I were dead.
¹³ *I have heard many insults.*
   Terror is all around me.
They make plans against me.
   They want to kill me.

¹⁴ *Lord, I trust you.*
   I have said, "You are my God."
¹⁵ *My life is in your hands.*
   Save me from my enemies' grasp.
   Save me from those who are chasing me.
¹⁶ *Show your kindness to me, your servant.*
   Save me because of your love.

Questions for us all

1. What can you spot from David's song that matches how you think Jesus felt? Underline it in the words above.

2. Did you spot the moment David's mood changed? What does he say that shows why he feels different? (If you're stuck, look at verse 14. In the NIV and ESV, this verse starts with "But...")

Question for 3s and 4s

How did King David feel in this song?

Question for 5-7s

David sang about his friends running away from him, afraid (verse 11). Can you remember when that happened to Jesus?

Question for over-7s

What is it that David knows and says to God when he is almost at the end (see verses 14-15)? Why do you think that helps him? Would it help you when you feel that everything is all too difficult?

Question for teens

Verses 14-16 are a prayer. Imagine Jesus praying this. Did his Father in heaven answer this prayer? Do you think you could you trust God like that?

Prayer suggestion

Thank God that Jesus did trust his heavenly Father with his life. Pray that we will learn to do the same.

Got time to chat?

Jesus helps us see how it is possible to be in a terrible place but still keep trusting our heavenly Father. When life really hurts, how does it help to be trusting God? But what about when the pain does not go away? Does it help then to trust God?

Something more for the adults?

Read all of Psalm 31, imagining it on the lips of Christ. Is there one verse that strikes you most? Why?

Key Story

DAY 25

He's gone!

Where are we going today?

Jesus had said he would rise from the dead. The women remembered this when they saw the empty tomb and heard the angels' words.

READY?

- **Optional!** Put together a tray of ten small objects from around your home. They can be anything—a piece of fruit, a spoon, a leaf, a coin, a pencil... Cover them with a towel, so the others can't see them.

- Open your Bible to **Luke 24 v 1-8** (or read the passage from page 85).

LET'S GO!

Pray: Dear Father, Jesus rising from the dead is the best news ever. Please help us to know and feel it today. Amen.

Perhaps try...

- Get out your covered tray of objects. Don't show the objects to your family yet. Instead, as you look at them, tell the others what the ten objects are. Then ask them to tell you back all ten objects. Can they remember what you said was on the tray? When they have remembered all that they can manage, show them the objects.

- Explain that in today's story some friends of Jesus are reminded of what Jesus had said to them, but they're only now remembering and understanding what he had said.

Passage

- *Where are we in the Bible?* We've reached *that* moment! On Friday evening just before sunset, Jesus' body was taken down from the cross and laid in an empty tomb with a stone rolled across the door. It's now Sunday morning and the sun is just coming up...

- *Look out* for the surprises. There are a few to spot!

- *Read* the passage.

Luke 24 v 1-8

[1] *Very early on the first day of the week, the women came to the tomb where Jesus' body was laid. They brought the spices they had prepared.* [2] *They found that the stone had been rolled away from the entrance of the tomb.* [3] *They went in, but they did not find the body of the Lord Jesus.* [4] *While they were wondering about this, two men in shining clothes suddenly stood beside them.* [5] *The women were very afraid; they bowed their heads to the ground. The men said to the women, "Why are you looking for a living person here? This is a place for the dead.* [6] *Jesus is not here. He has risen from death! Do you remember what he said in Galilee?* [7] *He said that the Son of Man must be given to evil men, be killed on a cross, and rise from death on the third day."* [8] *Then the women remembered what Jesus had said.*

Questions for us all

1. Which different shocks did you spot that surprised the group of women?

2. What did the "men in shining clothes" (they were angels) remind the women about? According to the angels, what had Jesus told them to expect? (Look at verses 6-7.) And which of these had already happened?

Question for 3s and 4s

Who did the women find at Jesus' tomb? What a shock!

Question for 5-7s

What job had God given the angels to do in this story?

Question for over-7s

If Jesus had already told the women to expect all of this, why do you think they were so surprised?

Question for teens

The angels could have just told the women what had happened. What difference did it make that Jesus had *already* told them it would happen?

Prayer suggestion

Thank Jesus for his perfect plan and his wonderful control of every detail. He is Lord indeed. What a King to have!

Got time to chat?

It is amazing that such a world-shaking event was announced by mighty angels to a small collection of women in a quiet corner of a graveyard. None of the women were important. Some of them had really embarrassing past lives. All of them would be completely forgotten by now except for this moment happening. What can we tell ourselves when we feel small, forgotten and unimportant?

Something more for the adults?

Read Luke 18 v 31-34. Now you can see why they hadn't remembered! "The meaning was hidden from them" (v 34). They couldn't have remembered. They couldn't have understood. They couldn't have made sense of these events. It was like trying to put together a complicated puzzle without a picture. It was a confusing and distressing mass of chaotic events. But now! Oh, the difference! Angels delivered the words of Christ. The Spirit of God would work in their memories, in their minds and in their hearts. Their lives would now flourish. Everything could now be seen in full, glorious, crystal-clear technicolour. If you see, understand and believe in the resurrection of Jesus Christ, then you have some prayers of praise and thanks to pray!

Key Story

DAY 26
Nonsense?

Where are we going today?

Jesus was alive! But his closest friend thought that this news was complete and utter rubbish...

READY?

- **Optional!** Find the sand art account of this story by searching for "Luke 24 sand art" in YouTube.
- Open your Bible to **Luke 24 v 9-12** (or read the passage from page 88).

LET'S GO!

Pray: Dear Father, please would we still be surprised and amazed by Jesus' resurrection—no matter how many times we have heard about it before. Amen.

Perhaps try...

- To recap yesterday's action, watch the beginning of the story told in sand art on *youtube*.

Passage

- *Where are we in the Bible?* The angels reminded the women at the tomb of Jesus' words when he was with them. The women remembered. Now what?
- *Look out* for what Jesus' closest friends thought of the women's story.
- *Read* the passage.

Luke 24 v 9-12

⁹ The women left the tomb and told all these things to the 11 apostles and the other followers. ¹⁰ These women were Mary Magdalene, Joanna, Mary the mother of James, and some other women. The women told the apostles everything that had happened at the tomb. ¹¹ But they did not believe the women. It sounded like nonsense. ¹² But Peter got up and ran to the tomb. He looked in, but he saw only the cloth that Jesus' body had been wrapped in. Peter went away to be alone, wondering about what had happened.

Questions for us all

1. What did the women tell the apostles? What did the apostles think of their story? (*Note: This passage calls Jesus' closest followers his apostles, but do say "disciples" if your children would find that easier.*)

2. How did Peter feel after he visited the tomb? Why do you think that was?

Question for 3s and 4s

Peter ran to the tomb where Jesus' body had been laid. Did Peter find Jesus' body there, inside the tomb?

Question for 5-7s

Why do you think Peter ran to the tomb?

Question for over-7s

What do you think Peter was thinking as he walked away from the tomb? What questions do you think he had? Can you think of three of them?

Question for teens

What was it about the resurrection story that seemed like nonsense to the disciples? Has that changed? Is it any harder or easier to believe it today?

Prayer suggestion

Is there someone you would like to pray for who thinks Jesus' resurrection is nonsense? Would you pray that they will look at the proof for themselves, just as Peter did.

Got time to chat?

It's not a surprise to us if people think that the Bible story is nonsense. Let's not be angry with them. Let's not give up. Let's not be discouraged. What will we say to ourselves when we find it discouraging? What makes us certain that the Bible story is true? What shall we pray for those people who still think it is nonsense?

Something more for the adults?

Read 1 Corinthians 1 v 26-31. We're not surprised thousands of years later when others look at us with pity (or anger) and tell us that Jesus Christ is a nonsense. God has always allowed the world to look at the evidence and say, "Nonsense". Others may look at the claims of the resurrection, seeing weakness and foolishness, and despising the empty tomb. But we see our hope, our strength and our future glory. We will for ever boast in the Lord.

DAY 27
Seen (but not recognised)

Where are we going today?

If Jesus is not alive, it would be so disappointing. Jesus was seen alive, but he stopped his friends from knowing it was him.

READY?

- **Do it if you can!** Get three sheets of paper and a felt-tip pen.
- Open your Bible to **Luke 24 v 13-24** (or read the passage from below).

LET'S GO!

Pray: Dear Jesus, please would you help us see the truth about you? We need you to do this. Amen.

Perhaps try...

- Splitting this passage into three sections, draw a very rough sketch for each part.
- These sketches really don't need to be great artworks. Their value is in giving something visual to focus on to simplify the story as you read through it.
- If the children are old enough, then they might be able to do the sketches themselves.
- Here is a rough plan of what could be drawn to represent each section. Do the drawing after reading each section.

SECTION	WHAT'S HAPPENING?	WHAT COULD YOU SKETCH?
V 13-14	Two friends are walking to Emmaus	
V 15-19	Jesus joins them. They are sad.	
V 20-24	The two friends explain the story so far.	

Passage

- *Where are we in the Bible?* The women found an empty tomb and two angels explaining that Jesus had said he would rise again. Jesus' disciples thought their stories were all nonsense, but the empty tomb amazed them. But no one had yet seen the risen Jesus...

- In this story, two of Jesus' friends meet Jesus but they don't know it is him. The Bible says that they were stopped from understanding that it was Jesus. Only God has the power to do that. So although they met Jesus, looked at him, talked to him and heard him talk—they didn't understand it was him.

- *Look out* for how these two friends felt as they left Jerusalem and walked to Emmaus.

- *Read* the passage.

Luke 24 v 13-24 (If using pictures, read this in three sections as shown below.)

¹³ That same day two of Jesus' followers were going to a town named Emmaus. It is about seven miles from Jerusalem. ¹⁴ They were talking about everything that had happened.

-----

¹⁵ While they were discussing these things, Jesus himself came near and began walking with them. ¹⁶ (They were not allowed to recognize Jesus.) ¹⁷ Then he said, "What are these things you are talking about while you walk?"

The two followers stopped. Their faces were very sad. ¹⁸ The one named Cleopas answered, "You must be the only one in Jerusalem who does not know what just happened there."

¹⁹ Jesus said to them, "What are you talking about?"

The followers said, "It is about Jesus of Nazareth. He was a prophet from God to all the people. He said and did many powerful things.

-----

²⁰ Our leaders and the leading priests gave him up to be judged and killed. They nailed him to a cross. ²¹ But we were hoping that he would free the Jews. It is now the third day since this happened. ²² And today some women among us told us some amazing things. Early this morning they went to the tomb, ²³ but they did not find his body there. They came and told us that they had seen a vision of angels. The angels said that Jesus was alive! ²⁴ So some of our group went to the tomb, too. They found it just as the women said, but they did not see Jesus."

Questions for us all (There's a question for each section.)

1. (v 13-14) What do you think the friends were saying to each other as they walked along?

2. (v 15-19) How did the two friends feel as Jesus walked up to them and spoke to them?

3. (v 20-24) What did the two friends think had happened to Jesus?

Question for 3s and 4s

(Whisper) Shh! This question is about a secret. Do you know who the man was who walked up to the two people on the road?

Question for 5-7s

Jesus didn't let them see who he was. What do you think they would have said or felt if they had known who he was?

Question for over-7s

As the friends explained what had happened to Jesus, what sort of person did they now think Jesus was? An ordinary guy? A special man sent from God? A liar? The Son of God? An amazing man? God's promised King?

Question for teens

The friends said that they'd hoped that Jesus would save Israel from the Roman Empire's occupation (verse 21). You can see why they were disappointed. Did Jesus die to do something *more* or *less* amazing than that?

Prayer suggestion

Thank God that Jesus has made himself clear to us. It's not a secret anymore! Thank God for what you find most exciting and amazing about Jesus.

Got time to chat?

There will be times when we feel totally disappointed. Perhaps everything feels as if it's gone wrong. It's likely in that moment that we have forgotten that Jesus has risen from the dead. We feel like the two friends—as if the Lord is dead and buried. In those moments, how would it change how you feel to remember that Jesus is walking alongside you—alive and ruling?

Something more for the adults?

Read 1 Corinthians 15 v 14-19. If Christ has not been raised, then we are downcast. Always. Every day. It's worth pondering just what we don't have without a risen Christ. We can understand why these two friends were deflated and disappointed, and without hope. That would be us. The value in pondering life without the risen Lord is that we can then fire ourselves up with the reality! *The Lord is risen.* See the difference that Christ's resurrection makes to every moment of your life.

DAY 28

Like a fire burning inside

Where are we going today?

The risen Jesus thrilled his friends by showing them that the whole Bible is about him.

READY?

- **Optional!** Can you find a small selection of items that represent *excitement* for your family? Perhaps a postcard from a great holiday, or a ticket to an event, or a picture of people you love to see, or a football, or a favourite electronic gadget?
- Open your Bible to **Luke 24 v 25-35** (or read the passage from page 95).

LET'S GO!

Pray: Dear Father, please help us to find learning more about Jesus so exciting that it feels like a fire burning inside us. Amen.

Perhaps try...

- Lay out the "exciting" objects in front of your family.
- Get different people to explain what each item is and why it might remind you of being excited.
- Can each member of the family describe what they could do this weekend that would be most exciting?
- Today we are going to find out what Jesus' friends thought was so exciting that it felt like a fire burning inside them.

Passage

- *Where are we in the Bible?* Two friends were walking from Jerusalem to Emmaus, when Jesus started walking with them. Jesus stopped them from seeing who he was, so they talked to him about how sad they felt about all that had happened to Jesus. They were so disappointed by his death. They hadn't understood Jesus' plan.

- *Look out* for what most excited the two friends in this story.

- *Read* the passage.

Luke 24 v 25-35

25 Then Jesus said to them, "You are foolish and slow to realise what is true. You should believe everything the prophets said. 26 They said that the Christ must suffer these things before he enters his glory." 27 Then Jesus began to explain everything that had been written about himself in the Scriptures. He started with Moses, and then he talked about what all the prophets had said about him.

28 They came near the town of Emmaus, and Jesus acted as if he did not plan to stop there. 29 But they begged him, "Stay with us. It is late; it is almost night." So he went in to stay with them.

30 Jesus sat down with them and took some bread. He gave thanks for the food and divided it. Then he gave it to them. 31 And then, they were allowed to recognise Jesus. But when they saw who he was, he disappeared. 32 They said to each other, "When Jesus talked to us on the road, it felt like a fire burning in us. It was exciting when he explained the true meaning of the Scriptures."

33 So the two followers got up at once and went back to Jerusalem. There they found the 11 apostles and others gathered. 34 They were saying, "The Lord really has risen from death! He showed himself to Simon."

35 Then the two followers told what had happened on the road. They talked about how they recognised Jesus when he divided the bread.

Questions for us all

1. Did you spot what the two friends were most excited about? What did they talk about first after Jesus disappeared? (Look in verse 32.)

2. What did Jesus want the two men to understand about the whole of the Bible? (Look in verse 27.)

Question for 3s and 4s

Listen for what happened to Jesus just after he broke the bread to share. (Read verses 30-31.)

Question for 5-7s

Jesus broke the bread. Suddenly the two friends realised that it was actually Jesus! But then he immediately disappeared. So many shocks and surprises. How would you have been feeling at that moment?

Question for over-7s

What was it about Jesus teaching the Bible that made them feel as if there was a fire burning inside them? Why would that be so exciting?

Question for teens

It's incredible that the two friends were more excited about being taught the Bible even than about meeting Jesus alive after he had been dead. Most of us think that if only we got to meet Jesus, we'd find easier to trust him. What would these two friends want to say to us about that?

Prayer suggestion

Pray that the Spirit would make our hearts burn with excitement when we read the Bible and see how Jesus is there the whole way through.

Got time to chat?

Reading the Bible can seem like the *last* thing we want to do. What does Jesus want us to understand about the Bible? Why does he think it's so exciting?

It's strange that Jesus wanted his discouraged friends to be taught the Bible before showing them that he had risen from the dead. He must have thought the Bible was more encouraging and wonderful even than meeting him. That's so helpful for us. We can't see Jesus, but we have the Bible too. So, when we're next discouraged about trusting Jesus, what will we tell ourselves?

Something more for the adults?

Read verses 31-32 again. Two discouraged, heartbroken friends. Eyes opened. Hearts burning. The resurrected Jesus spoke the truth to them, about himself, from the pages of the Bible. This is the normal Christian experience. We are frequently discouraged, heartbroken travellers on life's path. By his Spirit, the risen Christ walks alongside us, explaining his Bible to our burning hearts. Each day, we need this experience to keep going. Pray that this would be our story.

DAY 29

Given all power for ever

Where are we going today?

Jesus has been made the King over all people, for ever. He will never be beaten and will never die again. Daniel was allowed to see this in a dream.

READY?

- Look at the timeline on page 117 to see that, even though this dream was written down many years *before* Jesus, it is God explaining more about Jesus.

- **Optional!** Find a large piece of paper for your family to share, or a piece of paper for each family member with some felt-tip pens.

- Open your Bible to **Daniel 7 v 13-14** (or read the passage from page 98).

LET'S GO!

Pray: Dear Father, please help us to understand how Daniel prepared us for Jesus rising again. Amen.

Perhaps try...

- This is a vivid description of an epic moment in history. You, someone else or each person could draw (or scribble!) a sketch of what is being described, as one of you slowly reads the passage, one phrase at a time.

- The sketch might include "someone who looked like a human being" arriving in clouds, God's throne, some representation of power being handed over (a crown or a set of keys or a certificate), and many people worshipping.

- We're going to have to use our imaginations, as this picture language is mind-boggling!

Passage

- *Where are we in the Bible?* We were looking at the story of Jesus meeting his two friends on the road to Emmaus. Jesus had said that the promised King had to suffer first and then "enter his glory" (Luke 24 v 26). *Write "Entering his glory" at the top of each piece of paper.*

- 550 years before Jesus was born, Daniel was one of God's prophets. You may know about his adventure in the lion's den, but that's a small part of his amazing life. God gave Daniel a dream, showing him the day when a man would *enter glory*. Daniel didn't know he was watching Jesus Christ entering his glory. We do. "Glory" is the amazing, blinding beauty of God. It is a way to describe what we will see and feel when we meet God.

- *Look out* for what you think is happening here. The way it is described is strange.

- *Read* the passage.

Daniel 7 v 13-14

¹³ "In my vision at night I looked. There in front of me was someone who looked like a human being. He was coming with clouds in the sky. He came near God, who has been alive for ever. And he was led to God. ¹⁴ The one who looked like a human being was given the power to rule. He was also given glory and royal power. All peoples, nations and men who spoke every language will serve him. His rule will last for ever. His kingdom will never be destroyed.

Questions for us all

1. How did Daniel describe the person in his vision?

2. What did God give him? Can you make a list?

Question for 3s and 4s

Did you hear how Jesus travelled to God? Listen carefully as it's amazing! (Read verse 13.)

Question for 5-7s

Daniel saw Jesus being made the King by God. How does this dream say Jesus will be different to any other king who has ever lived?

Question for over-7s

As you look at what God gave Jesus (verse 14), which do you find the most surprising item on your list? Do you find it hard to believe that any of these gifts are true of Jesus?

Question for teens

In Luke 24 v 26 Jesus said that "the Christ must suffer these things before he enters his glory". According to Daniel's dream, Jesus *right now* has all power and authority. Do you see or hear any evidence of this in the world today?

Prayer suggestion

Jesus rose to enjoy his power as King for ever. Let's pray that we will know how powerful Jesus is and believe in him. What a King to have in charge!

Got time to chat?

Jesus' power is hard to believe, particularly if you look around the world today. For a King who is ruling over every person in every country, very few people seem to be talking about him. That is sad. What is helpful to remember from Daniel's vision when we find it hard to believe that the risen Jesus really is ruling?

Something more for the adults?

Read Matthew 28 v 18-20. Jesus himself confirms that Daniel's vision has happened. It's history. It's real. *All power and authority* has been given to Jesus by God. There is nothing outside of his power. What, does Jesus say, is the obvious result of him having all this power? This is a helpful motivation when we find it a struggle to speak to others about Christ. Our King is enthroned. He has all power. All people will one day fall at his feet and worship. There will never be a day, ever, when he is not ruling. Let's not keep that to ourselves!

DAY 30

Seen, touched and fed

Where are we going today?

Jesus showed his friends his scars and he ate food to prove that it was really him. In heaven, we will have bodies just like Jesus' body.

READY?

- **Optional!** Gather a few items from your kitchen and home that can be seen, tasted, smelt, touched and heard. Put them on a tray under a cover. Ideas:

  - *Touch:* Practically any object, as long as it is not sharp. For example, a coin, a spoon or a toy.

  - *Sight:* Can you find one obscure small part of an object so the children can guess what it belongs to? Use a lid, a tool or a kitchen utensil wrapped almost entirely in a kitchen towel.

  - *Taste:* With eyes shut, can you taste a few different fruits, crisps or drinks.

  - *Smell:* Find any distinctive-smelling foods—coffee, fruit, spices—or cleaning products.

  - Hear: Choose something that you can shake, such as a box of cereal or a packet of potato crisps.

- Open your Bible to **Luke 24 v 36-43** (or read the passage from page 101).

LET'S GO!

Pray: Dear Father, please help us to understand what we and Jesus will be like in heaven. Amen.

Perhaps try...

- To introduce today's key idea, use your five senses to identify various items.

- In today's story, we are going to see that Jesus told his friends to use their senses to be sure it really was him.

Passage

- *Where are we in the Bible?* The women found Jesus' tomb empty. The angels explained that Jesus was alive. Two friends met a mystery man on their way to Emmaus, but as soon as they realised it was Jesus, he disappeared. Those two ran back to Jesus' other friends to tell them everything. Will anyone get to just see Jesus and talk to him... normally?

- *Look out* for how many different senses Jesus tells his friends to use to check that it really was him.

- *Read* the passage.

Luke 24 v 36-43

36 While the two followers were telling this, Jesus himself stood among those gathered. He said to them, "Peace be with you."

37 They were fearful and terrified. They thought they were seeing a ghost. 38 But Jesus said, "Why are you troubled? Why do you doubt what you see? 39 Look at my hands and my feet. It is I myself! Touch me. You can see that I have a living body; a ghost does not have a body like this."

40 After Jesus said this, he showed them his hands and feet. 41 The followers were amazed and very happy. They still could not believe it. Jesus said to them, "Do you have any food here?" 42 They gave him a piece of cooked fish. 43 While the followers watched, Jesus took the fish and ate it.

Questions for us all

1. How did the disciples feel when Jesus was suddenly standing among them? Why do you think that was?

2. Jesus knew that they were worried and confused. How did he help them?

Question for 3s and 4s

What did they give Jesus to eat? (Read verses 41-43.)

Question for 5-7s

Which senses did Jesus use to show his friends that it really was him? *(To make this easier, go through each sense and ask if Jesus used that one to show that it was really him.)*

Question for over-7s

What did Jesus want his friends to be absolutely certain of? Are you certain that it really was Jesus alive in the room? Or do you find it hard, as the disciples did?

Question for teens

When people think about heaven, they often seem to think about clouds and harps. Or people worry that their imperfect bodies will still be who they are. How does this story help us understand what our bodies will be like when we rise from the dead, in heaven? How do you feel about that?

Prayer suggestion

Thank Jesus for what you feel certain about. Tell Jesus what you find confusing or hard to understand.

Got time to chat?

Even after the disciples had seen, heard and touched Jesus, they were still finding it hard to believe it was Jesus because they were "amazed and very happy". What is there that still fills you with joy and amazement about Jesus being alive? We can get so used to the story of the first Easter that we forget the joy and amazement. It's worth taking a moment to find it again. When Easter has become dull and boring, we have stopped understanding it.

Something more for the adults?

Read 1 Corinthians 15 v 51-57. There will be a moment, for every Christian, when the trumpet will sound and we will be raised imperishable, indestructible, immortal. We will be different to how we are now. But we will be us. Wonderfully us. Perfectly us. Without sin. Without disability. Without frustration. Without death. Thanks be to God. He gives us the victory through our Lord Jesus Christ!

A note about Jesus' resurrection body

After Jesus had risen from the dead, he seemed to be like any other person: he walked, talked and had the scars from his death. But he was also different. People couldn't tell it was him; he could just disappear and then appear somewhere else. In today's story we see more of how normal and how different Jesus now is.

Key
Story

DAY 31

You must tell people

Where are we going today?

God's plan was always for Jesus to die and rise again—and then for his followers to explain Jesus' forgiveness to others.

READY?

- **Do it if you can!** Get a single large piece of paper and some felt-tip pens to draw God's mega-plan for the universe. Grab a pair of scissors.
- Open your Bible to **Luke 24 v 44-49** (or read the passage from page 104).

LET'S GO!

Pray: Dear Father, please help us to understand your big plan for the universe. Please help us to see our part in your big plan. Amen.

Perhaps try...

- Today's passage is a conversation about concepts. A single visual will help children to grasp the big idea.
- Verse 45 tells us that Jesus helped his friends to understand the whole message of the Bible. Verses 46-48 *are* the whole message of the Bible: God's mega-plan for the universe! It's a three-step plan. See page 105 for a simple outline to draw as you read the passage.

Passage

- *Where are we in the Bible?* Jesus has suddenly appeared in a room where his disciples are gathered. They are so excited, amazed and confused that Jesus has to prove that it really is him. Now that they realise that it is him, what will he say to them?

- *Look out* for what Jesus wants them, and us, to understand before he leaves and returns to heaven.

- *Read* the passage.

Luke 24 v 44-49

⁴⁴ He said to them, "Remember when I was with you before? I said that everything written about me must happen—everything in the law of Moses, the books of the prophets, and the Psalms."

⁴⁵ Then Jesus opened their minds so they could understand the Scriptures. ⁴⁶ He said to them, "It is written that the Christ would be killed and rise from death on the third day. ⁴⁷⁻⁴⁸ You saw these things happen— you are witnesses. You must tell people to change their hearts and lives. If they do this, their sins will be forgiven. You must start at Jerusalem and preach these things in my name to all nations. ⁴⁹ Listen! My Father has promised you something; I will send it to you. But you must stay in Jerusalem until you have received that power from heaven."

Questions for us all

1. Read verse 45 again. What do you think Jesus is doing when it says, "Jesus opened their minds so they could understand the Scriptures"?

2. Can the children see the three parts of God's mega-plan in verses 46-48? The Christ **would be killed**, he **would rise from death** and **you must tell people**. What does each of these three parts mean?

   (If you haven't drawn the plan out, then point to each of the three parts opposite in turn. If you've drawn the mega-plan onto a piece of paper, now cut it up into the three parts. Which of these three parts have happened? Which of these three parts is still happening?)

For under-7s, you can simplify this picture to Cross > Empty tomb > Speech bubble.

For over-7s, you can include in the speech bubble the three truths that Jesus wants us to explain to others.

GOD'S MEGA-PLAN FOR THE UNIVERSE

1. The King must be killed

2. The King must rise from death

3. You must tell people...

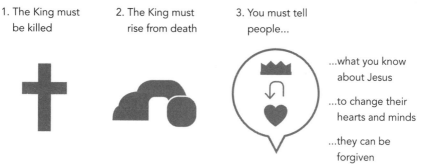

...what you know about Jesus

...to change their hearts and minds

...they can be forgiven

Question for 3s and 4s

Jesus told his friends that they had seen everything he had done. Now they had to tell others about him. What do *you* want to tell others about Jesus?

Question for 5-7s

Jesus says that his disciples are witnesses of these things. What have they seen? What do you think they need to tell others about him?

Question for over-7s

When Jesus says that they must preach these things, he means that they, and we, have to tell others about these things. What must we tell others? Can you practise on me?

Question for teens

It can feel as if Jesus has left us the hardest part of the plan to complete. But verse 49 says he's about to send the secret weapon to make it possible. How does the Holy Spirit help *you* to tell others?

Prayer suggestion

You could thank Jesus for the parts of the mega-plan that he's completed—and pray for the parts that he wants us to be involved with. Ask for the help of the Spirit.

Got time to chat?

The mega-plan often feels a long way removed from normal, everyday life. It can help us to spot which of the three steps we could think about when we find everyday life to be hard. Shall I think about Jesus' death, which means I'm forgiven and in his family? Shall I think about Jesus' resurrection, which means he is ruling and gives me hope for heaven? Shall I think about telling others, which means they need to know how they can be fixed, loved, joyful and full of hope?

Something more for the adults?

"Clothed with power from on high" (verse 49, NIV). Let's meditate on that. Every Christian, without exception, has been clothed with the power of the Spirit (Romans 8 v 9-11). If we haven't, then we're not a Christian. If we're a Christian, then we have. It's a promise. What a blessing if the Spirit is helping us to understand these things, helping us to pray, giving us some measure of joy as we open these verses with children; and if we can look forward to seeing Jesus eye to eye as the disciples did. To be a Christian is to be a new creation, to be sealed with the down-payment of heaven. To be a Christian is to be safe. Thank Christ if you are clothed with power from on high.

DAY 32

He's gone
We're still happy

Where are we going today?

Jesus left his friends to join his Father in heaven. His friends were so joyful that they didn't stop singing songs to Jesus.

READY?

- **Optional!** Find something precious, something expensive or a treat that your family love.

- Open your Bible to **Luke 24 v 50-53** (or read the passage from page 108).

LET'S GO!

Pray: Dear Father, saying goodbye can be difficult. Please teach us why Jesus' disciples were delighted despite saying goodbye to him. Please would we be just as delighted even though we can't see Jesus! Amen.

Perhaps try...

- Play a quick-fire game of hide and seek with your precious item.

- When something matters to us, we need to know where it is. We don't need to have it with us, but we need to know exactly where it is. When we don't know where it is, we find that very worrying. It's lost.

- In today's Bible passage, Jesus' disciples knew that they would no longer be able to see Jesus—but they knew exactly where he would be, so they were happy.

Passage

- *Where are we in the Bible?* Jesus had finished what he needed to do on earth: he had been killed and raised to life. Now his friends are absolutely certain he is alive and they know what to do next: to tell others. They are ready for Jesus to leave them.

- *Look out* for what the disciples did *first* after saying goodbye to Jesus.

- *Read* the passage.

Luke 24 v 50-53

⁵⁰ *Jesus led his followers out of Jerusalem almost to Bethany. He raised his hands and blessed them.* ⁵¹ *While he was blessing them, he was separated from them and carried into heaven.* ⁵² *They worshipped him and then went back to the city very happy.* ⁵³ *They stayed in the Temple all the time, praising God.*

Questions for us all

1. What was the last thing Jesus did for his friends before he left them?

2. What did the disciples do first after seeing Jesus leave?

Have you got time to sing a praise song to Jesus; just as the disciples did after he left them?

Question for 3s and 4s

How did Jesus leave?

Question for 5-7s

What do you think the disciples saw as Jesus left them? When they got home to their families that night, what do you think they said?

Question for over-7s

It's strange that when Jesus died, his friends were all super-miserable and sad. This time, when they know they won't get to see him, they're super-happy and shouty. Why do they feel so different? What has changed?

Question for teens

It's amazing to think that Jesus was sent to be executed for saying that he would sit down on the throne at God's right-hand side (Luke 22 v 69-71), and now he is off to do exactly that! The disciples left very happy and went to the temple, praising God all the time. Is there anything in this passage that makes you very happy, wanting to praise God all the time?

Prayer suggestion

There was huge joy for Jesus' friends in knowing that he left earth and went to rule, seated at the right-hand side of God on his glorious throne. Can you find one reason each to thank and praise God that Jesus is ruling with him?

Got time to chat?

Joy is what we all want, but we find it hard to be joyful for long. Joy is a deep sense that everything is just right. Deep in your guts, everything just feels that it's how God made it to be. Everything is alright. It is going to be alright. We don't need to be worried. The disciples managed to feel joyful for days, as they stayed at the temple, all day every day, hour after hour, praising God. Think for a moment about where that joy came from. They were convinced that Jesus was alive. He was real. He was never going to die again. He was on his throne. He was ruling. No one could ever stop him ruling. He was ruling over them. They were safe. They were his. He was there. Nothing else really mattered to them.

We too can feel that joy in our lowest moments. The lowest moments are still real. They still hurt. We still wish they weren't happening. But when we're in those moments, what will we say to ourselves, to remind ourselves of the deep, settled, unchanging joy that the disciples had, and that we can too?

Something more for the adults?

Luke didn't stop here. He pulled out a second parchment and started all over again. Read Acts 1 v 1-11 for Luke's second bite at the apple, where he retells these same events with a slightly different emphasis. Take a long look at verse 11. There are more reasons here for joy, expectation and hope. Imagine the day when some different people will look up and see Jesus Christ return. He will come down. His feet will come to gently rest on the earth once more and he will wrap all history up. You can feel joy as you look forward to that day. He's coming soon!

DAY 33

Very good Friday

Where are we going today?

Today we celebrate Jesus' death as "good" because his death brought us into his family.

READY?

- No kit needed!
- Open your Bible to **Luke 23 v 36-38** (or read the passage from page 111).

LET'S GO!

Pray: Dear Father, we don't normally celebrate a death, so please help us to understand why Good Friday is actually good. Amen.

Perhaps try...

- **Optional!** Each of you complete the sentence, "If I was the king for today, I would…"
- If any of you need help, ask: What would you choose to wear? What would you want to eat? How would you want others to speak to you? What would you want to do today?
- Today is Good Friday. On the first Good Friday, *Jesus* was the King. Remember how he chose to spend it?

Passage

- *Where are we in the Bible?* We're back at the first Good Friday. It's that moment when no one could understand how Jesus could be a king.

- *Look out* for the different ways Jesus is mentioned as the King.

- *Read* the passage.

Luke 23 v 36-38

[36] *Even the soldiers made fun of him. They came to Jesus and offered him some vinegar.* [37] *They said, "If you are the king of the Jews, save yourself!"* [38] *(At the top of the cross these words were written: "THIS IS THE KING OF THE JEWS.")*

Questions for us all

1. Can we find different ways people made fun of Jesus?

2. What did they tell Jesus to do?

Question for 3s and 4s

Everyone was shouting horrible things at Jesus. How do you think Jesus was feeling?

Question for 5-7s

Could Jesus have got himself off the cross? Why didn't he?

Question for over-7s

Why did the soldiers think a king should save himself? So what sort of king is Jesus?

Question for teens

The Romans were having a laugh at Jesus and the Jews. It must have looked ridiculous to have "This is the king" written above a bleeding, mostly naked dying man. As you imagine looking at this king on the cross, how do you feel?

Prayer suggestion

Imagine Jesus walked in right now and sat down next to you. What would you say to him?

Got time to chat?

How is Good Friday *good*? Can you think of a better name for it?

Something more for the adults?

Read Philippians 2 v 8-11. This is the description of your King. God's assessment is the only assessment that matters. What is God's assessment of his King? Pray in response to your meditation on these verses.

Key Story

DAY 34

Oh happy day!

Where are we going today?

Happy Easter! Our King Jesus is risen. Everything is now better.

READY?

- **Optional!** You might like to do one of the following:
  - EITHER: Grab one of those foiled-covered hollow chocolate Easter eggs that has nothing inside.
  - OR: Blow the contents out of a real egg. You can do this by making a small hole in each end using a sharp knife or a skewer. Then blow (long and hard) from one end and the egg contents will come out of the other end. Be careful not to swallow any of the raw egg. Wash your mouth afterwards.
- Open your Bible to **Luke 24 v 1-8** (or read the passage from page 114).

LET'S GO!

Pray: Dear Father, please can you help us to discover that the Bible is more exciting than any chocolate or Easter presents can be? Amen.

Perhaps try...

- *Either* take the Easter egg out of its box, and then very slowly take off the foil; *or* show the blown egg to your family.
- What do each of you think is inside the egg? Break it open. Show the inside to your family.

- An empty egg is disappointing. But the empty tomb is the most exciting thrill in the history of the world!

Passage

- *Where are we in the Bible?* Today is Easter Sunday. Let's go back to the first Easter Sunday, and remember why we're still celebrating it 2000 years later.

- *Look out* for what the women were going to do at the tomb.

- *Read* the passage.

Luke 24 v 1-8

[1] *Very early on the first day of the week, the women came to the tomb where Jesus' body was laid. They brought the spices they had prepared.* [2] *They found that the stone had been rolled away from the entrance of the tomb.* [3] *They went in, but they did not find the body of the Lord Jesus.* [4] *While they were wondering about this, two men in shining clothes suddenly stood beside them.* [5] *The women were very afraid; they bowed their heads to the ground. The men said to the women, "Why are you looking for a living person here? This is a place for the dead.* [6] *Jesus is not here. He has risen from death! Do you remember what he said in Galilee?* [7] *He said that the Son of Man must be given to evil men, be killed on a cross, and rise from death on the third day."* [8] *Then the women remembered what Jesus had said.*

Questions for us all

1. What did the women expect to find? What did they come to do?

2. What did they know when they left that they didn't know before?

Question for 3s and 4s

What did the women see when they arrived at the tomb?

Question for 5-7s

What did the angels come to tell them?

Question for over-7s

The angels reminded the women of what Jesus had said—that he would rise again on the third day. If they had remembered what Jesus said about rising again, what do you think they might have done differently?

Question for teens

Today we celebrate that Jesus is alive. What has Jesus' resurrection fixed for you?

Prayer suggestion

We are celebrating the greatest day in history. What do you want to thank God for? Think for a moment. What is there that is new, or wonderful, or surprising, or life-changing? There are so many answers. Pick a few.

Got time to chat?

While we eat a little too much chocolate, or hot cross buns, or Easter cake, we can ask each other, "Why is today the greatest day in history?"

Something more for the adults?

How do you respond to the resurrection? Do you see it as a happy ending to what would otherwise have been a tragic tale? Or as the truth that changes you from being dead in sin to alive in Christ? Of all days, today is the day to take just a few extra minutes to ponder a verse and to pray in response: perhaps Luke 24 verse 6 or verse 39.

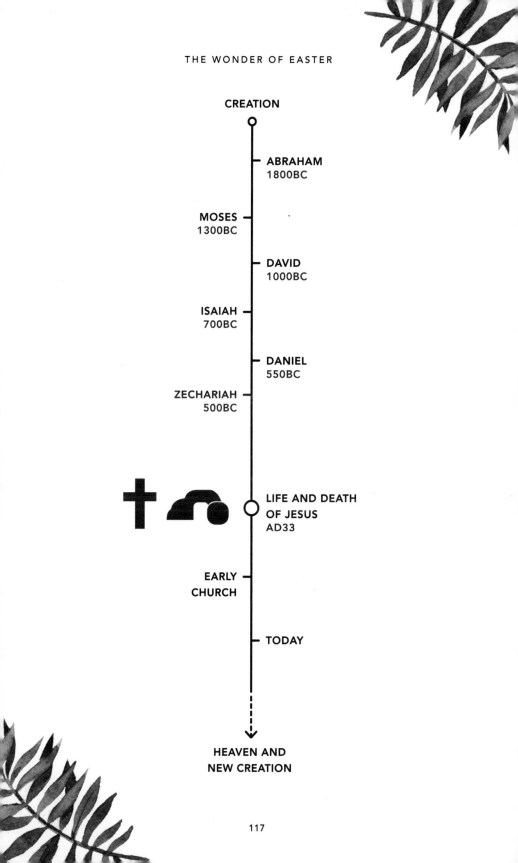

CREATION

ABRAHAM
1800BC

MOSES
1300BC

DAVID
1000BC

ISAIAH
700BC

DANIEL
550BC

ZECHARIAH
500BC

LIFE AND DEATH
OF JESUS
AD33

EARLY
CHURCH

TODAY

HEAVEN AND
NEW CREATION

Top tips

- A hardback Bible sits open, flat on a table, so it is one less thing to go wrong or to distract children by flicking shut. For under-11s, the International Children's Bible is a good, simplified version. This is the version we have printed in this book. Otherwise the New International Version is great. For a large family, each person will need their own Bible, using the same translation, or their own copy of this book. Alternatively, in whatever translation you choose, you could print out copies of the passage from www.biblegateway.com

- Under-5s will struggle with many of the activities. They find it hard to understand that a drama is recreating an ancient story. They find metaphors, illustrations and visual aids hard to process. This age-group would be helped by having a children's picture Bible to see what is happening in the Bible stories. *The Beginners Bible* and the *Jesus Storybook Bible* are good for this. These devotions will need to be kept very simple for them.

- Try to read through the devotion once, before you sit down with your children. Often, it will help if you grab a suggested object as a prop before you start. Occasionally, there is the option to prepare a visual aid.

- If your family are new to devotions, or if you are re-starting them after a break, and you face some opposition to the idea, you could set a ten-minute timer (and hide it, so that the ticking seconds aren't watched!). Promise that when the alarm goes off, you will stop the conversation and all present will pray in response. Keep that promise—no matter how far you've got.

- If your children are currently more malleable, then don't set a timer, as it may set an expectation that the ten minutes will be a form of a torture.

- Do set an expectation that this time together will be the highlight of the day. Jesus talked about the Bible as "daily bread"—your family needs this ten minutes each day to survive.

- Remember that there is huge value in your children seeing their parents answering questions from the Bible, talking about their faith, showing that they don't have all the answers and praying. It will have a lasting impact for children to see their parents engaging with the Bible, humbly accepting that they themselves are a work in progress and praying to their own Father in heaven.

- Many families are clinging on to sanity, joy, peace, hope or faith by their fingernails. Ask for your children to help make these happen.

  - What time do we want these devotions to happen?

  - Where do we want them to happen so that they will be a great opportunity to learn and concentrate?

  - What will need to be done before we can sit down together each day?

  - What role can each of us play to make them happen?

  - Don't be disappointed if these devotions feel like ten minutes of slightly miserable chaos. If you can manage to do three or four so that there is a sense of an expectation and a routine, then things will usually improve. As always with children, there will be days that leave you in despair. Those days will show you your need of Jesus Christ in your parenting. No bad thing.

- Change the plan if the plan isn't working.

- God bless you in this. Take a moment to pray for your efforts. If you don't already feel dependent on Jesus Christ in your parenting, you are about to!

Get your family excited about a Jesus Christmas

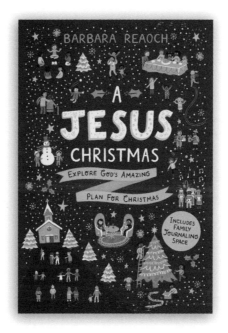

This Advent devotional offers a fresh way for your family to prepare for Christmas. Right from the beginning, the serpent lied to Adam and Eve in the Garden of Eden—and he has been lying ever since. But right from the beginning, God told us his amazing plan to send Jesus.

Each of the 25 readings looks at one of the serpent's lies, and then shows how Jesus destroys it. This is followed by questions for children aged 4-11. There is even space to make your own notes. Prepare yourselves to celebrate Christmas in a new and lasting way with this innovative new resource.

thegoodbook.com/a-jesus-christmas
thegoodbook.co.uk/a-jesus-christmas

Bible-reading for every age and stage

Explore
(for adults)

Engage
(for 14+)

Discover
(for 11-13s)

XTB
(for 7-10s)

Table Talk
(for families)

Beginning with God
(for pre-schoolers)

thegoodbook.com/subscriptions
thegoodbook.co.uk/subscriptions